French

Harriette Lanzer

Published by BBC Worldwide Ltd,
80 Wood Lane, London W12 0TT

First published 2002 Reprinted June 2004

ISBN: 0 563 50124 3

Colour reproduction by Tien Wah Press Pte Ltd, Singapore

Printed and bound by Tien Wah Press Pte Ltd, Singapore

Acknowledgements
Photographs: © Honsingers

Contents

Young person in society

Listening

Exam questions and model answers

Exam instructions

Topic checker

Complete the grammar

Answers

Last-minute learner

Introduction

Using this book to revise

About Bitesize

GCSE Bitesize is a revision service designed to help you achieve success at GCSE. There are books, television programmes and a website, each of which provides a separate resource designed to help you get the best results.

TV programmes are available on video through your school or you can find out transmission times by calling 08700 100 222.

The website can be found at http://www.bbc.co.uk/schools/gcsebitesize/

About this book

This book is your all-in-one revision companion for GCSE.
It gives you the three things you need for successful revision:

1 **Every topic clearly organised and explained in four main chapters:** My world, Holiday time and travel, Work and lifestyle and Young person in society.

2 **The key vocabulary and grammar pulled out for quick and easy revision reference:** both in the four main chapters and in the extra sections at the end of the book.

3 **All the practice you need:** in the 'check' questions in the margins, in the practice questions at the end of each topic area, and in the exam practice section at the end of this book.

Each chapter is organised in the same way:

■ **Key vocabulary and phrases** broken down into smaller topic areas, with suggestions for learning the vocabulary and activities to practise it

■ **The Bare Bones** – a summary of the main points – a good way to check what you know

■ **Key ideas** highlighted throughout

■ **Check questions** in the margin – have you understood this bit?

About this book continued

- **Grammar boxes** highlighting the key grammar you need to know

- **Remember tips** in the margin – extra advice on this section of the topic

- **Practice questions** at the end of each topic to check your understanding

The extra sections at the back of this book will help you check your progress and be confident that you know your stuff:

- **Listening** – a chapter of listening activities which you can do if you have a copy of the Bitesize French video (see facing page for details of how to get it).

- **Exam questions and model answers** – example exam questions for Listening, Speaking, Reading and Writing – with model answers to help you get full marks.

- **Topic checker** – quick-fire questions on all your topics. See how many you can answer after you've revised a chapter and then check the answers back in the book.

- **Complete the grammar** – another resource for you to use as you revise: fill in the gaps to complete the key grammar.

- **Last-minute learner** – a mini-book that you can cut out containing all the most important vocabulary and phrases in just six pages.

- **Answers** – check all your answers to the activities in the book.

Planning your revision

You will be entered for examination at one of two levels: Foundation or Higher. The **(h)** symbol in this book indicates the information and questions that only need to be covered by Higher level entrants. Check with your teacher which level you will be expected to do and also which topics are included in your syllabus – there may be some topics in this book that you don't need to cover.

You will be entered for a Listening, Speaking, Reading and Writing exam (unless you're doing the written coursework option). Your revision needs to be planned in advance – it's no good leaving it all to the week before the exam, so a good idea is to write an action plan for yourself first of all. Once you've drawn up your revision timetable, you can start your actual work. When you revise, make sure that:

■ you've got a quiet place to work

■ you've got everything you need in the room – books, pens, paper, the video

■ you don't get distracted by computer games, the TV, radio, magazines ...

■ you don't revise for too long without a break – set a time limit for yourself to make sure that you keep fresh and motivated

On the day

Make sure that you know the exact day, time and place for each of your French exams. Get to the exam room in good time and make sure that you've got a pen and a pencil with you. On your way to the exam, go through a few key points in French – for instance, you could count to 50, say a few things about yourself or listen to a French cassette. Nobody expects you to know everything on the day of your exam, but see if you can manage to do the following:

■ **check that you know the French exam instructions (see page 98)**

■ **say two or three sentences about yourself in French**

■ **know your numbers to fifty (and above if possible)**

■ **know some dates and times**

■ **know some important key phrases**

The French exam

Here are a few suggestions to help you in the exam:

- When you get into the exam, **don't panic**. Have a quick look through the **whole paper** to see what you have to do.

- Don't spend too long on one section and not have time to finish all the sections.

- If something seems too difficult, leave it and continue with other questions – you can always come back later.

- **Don't leave gaps.** You cannot gain any marks if you don't give an answer.

- **Read carefully** what you have to do in each question, i.e. tick **four** boxes, answer in **English**, answer in **French**. You may lose marks if you don't read and follow the instructions carefully (see page 98 for a list of exam instructions).

- Remember that the exam gives you an opportunity to show the examiner what you know, understand and can do – so try and do just that!

A   Name and age

Comment t'appelles-tu?		What's your name?
Je m'appelle (Marc Brun).		My name is/I'm called (Marc Brun).
Comment ça s'écrit?		How do you spell that?
Ça s'écrit B.R.U.N.		That's spelled B.R.U.N.
Quel âge as-tu?		How old are you?
J'ai quinze/seize ans.		I'm fifteen/sixteen years old.

zéro	0	neuf	9	dix-huit	18	vingt-sept	27
un	1	dix	10	dix-neuf	19	vingt-huit	28
deux	2	onze	11	vingt	20	vingt-neuf	29
trois	3	douze	12	vingt et un	21	trente	30
quatre	4	treize	13	vingt-deux	22	trente et un	31
cinq	5	quatorze	14	vingt-trois	23	trente-deux	32
six	6	quinze	15	vingt-quatre	24	quarante	40
sept	7	seize	16	vingt-cinq	25	cinquante	50
huit	8	dix-sept	17	vingt-six	26	soixante	60

Q Cover the French column in these sections and look at the English. Write the French down. Check that you've got it all right and make any spelling corrections.

B   Birthdays

Mon anniversaire est le (sept février).	My birthday is on (7th February).
Je suis né(e) le (six janvier).	I was born on (6th January).
le premier (mai)	1st (May)
en deux mille cinq	in two thousand and five

janvier	*January*	mai	*May*	septembre	*September*
février	*February*	juin	*June*	octobre	*October*
mars	*March*	juillet	*July*	novembre	*November*
avril	*April*	août	*August*	décembre	*December*

Q Cover this section and write down all the months of the year with the letter 'e' in them.

C   Nationalities

Je suis anglais(e)/français(e). *I'm English/French.*			
britannique	*British*	écossais(e)	*Scottish*
irlandais(e)	*Irish*	gallois(e)	*Welsh*
allemand(e)	*German*	espagnol(e)	*Spanish*
italien(ne)	*Italian*	suisse	*Swiss*
américain(e)	*American*	canadien(ne)	*Canadian*

Remember
To form the feminine of an adjective you usually add 'e' to the masculine.

Grammar – adjective agreements

boy	Il est français. Il est petit/grand/gros.
girl	Elle est française. Elle est petite/grande/grosse.

My world

D Appearance

Q What do you look like? Describe yourself in three sentences.

J'ai les yeux bleus/verts/bruns.	*I've got blue/green/brown eyes.*
J'ai les cheveux bruns/marron.	*I've got brown/chestnut brown hair.*
J'ai les cheveux blonds/noirs.	*I've got blond/black hair.*
J'ai les cheveux raides.	*I've got straight hair.*
J'ai les cheveux frisés.	*I've got curly hair.*
J'ai les cheveux longs/courts.	*I've got long/short hair.*
J'ai une barbe.	*I've got a beard.*
Je porte des lunettes.	*I wear glasses.*
Je suis petit(e)/mince.	*I'm small/slim.*
Je suis grand(e)/gros(se).	*I'm tall/fat.*

E Pets

J'ai un chien/chat. *I've got a dog/cat.*

un cochon d'Inde	*guinea pig*	un cheval	*horse*
un hamster	*hamster*	une perruche	*budgie*
un oiseau	*bird*	une souris	*mouse*
un poisson rouge	*goldfish*	une tortue	*tortoise*
un lapin	*rabbit*		

Grammar – regular verb endings

	'er' verb – porter (*to wear*)	'ir' verb – finir (*to finish*)	're' verb attendre (*to wait*)
je	porte	finis	j'attends
tu	portes	finis	attends
il/elle/on	porte	finit	attend
nous	portons	finissons	attendons
vous	portez	finissez	attendez
ils/elles	portent	finissent	attendent

PRACTICE

Learn the French alphabet so you can spell words and names in the exam.
Have a go first with your name and the town where you live.

a	ah	**h**	ahsh	**o**	oh	**v**	vay
b	baye	**i**	ee	**p**	pay	**w**	doobler vay
c	say	**j**	zhee	**q**	kew	**x**	eeks
d	day	**k**	kah	**r**	ehr	**y**	ee grehk
e	eh	**l**	ehl	**s**	ehss	**z**	zehd
f	ehf	**m**	ehm	**t**	tay		
g	zhay	**n**	ehn	**u**	ewe		

My world

All about me

THE BARE BONES

➤ Make sure you can give information about yourself, such as name, age and appearance.

➤ Be prepared to do role plays about other people.

➤ Know your numbers in French.

A Personal details

SPEAK

1 In the speaking exam, the examiner will want to know a few things about you. He or she will probably ask you a few general questions about yourself to start the exam off, so **make sure you go in with ready answers.**

2 **Répondez aux questions. Answer the questions, using the details on the right.**

Exemple:

– Comment vous appelez-vous?   – Je m'appelle *Stephanie Waite.*

– Comment ça s'écrit, Waite?   – W.A.I.T.E. *(doobler vay. ah. ee. tay. ehr.)*

– Quelle est la date de votre anniversaire?   – C'est le *douze janvier.*

– Quel âge avez-vous?   – J'ai *dix-sept* ans.

– Quelle est votre nationalité?   – Je suis *anglaise.*

– Est-ce que vous avez des animaux?   – Oui, j'ai *un chien et un chat.*

details

• name – John Nugent

• birthday – 16th June

• 15 years old

• Scottish

• mouse and a guinea pig

Q Now answer the six questions for yourself. Write your answers down and learn them off by heart.

B Personal descriptions

WRITE

1 You are going to describe your appearance next – can you already describe your **eye colour, hair colour and style and body size?** Check on the vocabulary page 9 if you are not sure.

2 **Décrivez ces personnes. Describe the people as if they were you.**

Exemple: a Je m'appelle Paul et j'ai seize ans. J'ai les yeux bleus et les cheveux courts et bruns. Je suis mince et je porte des lunettes.

a   bleu   Paul   16

b   bleu   Béatrice   14

c   vert   Susanne   15

My world

Grammar – avoir and être

avoir		être	
j'ai (*I have*) tu as (*you have*) il/elle a (*he/she has*)	nous avons (*we have*) vous avez (*you have*) ils/elles ont (*they have*)	je suis (*I am*) tu es (*you are*) il/elle est (*he/she is*)	nous sommes (*we are*) vous êtes (*you are*) ils/elles sont (*they are*)

C   An ID form

WRITE

1 You might have to **fill in a form with personal information** in the exam, so have a look at the headings below and check you understand what you are being asked for.

2   **Complétez le formulaire. Fill in this ID form with details about yourself.**

> garçon ☐   fille ☐   célibataire ☐   marié(e) ☐
>
> **1** Prénom et nom de famille: _____   **2** Nationalité: _____
>
> **3** Adresse (avec code postal): _____
>
> **4** Numéro de téléphone: _____
>
> **5** Age: _____   **6** Anniversaire: _____
>
> **7** Animaux: _____
>
> **8** Cheveux/yeux: _____   **9** Taille/poids: _____

Q Can you work out what **célibataire** means?

PRACTICE

Use the information from the ID form above to write full sentences about yourself.

1 Je m'appelle   _____

2 Je suis   _____

3 J'habite _____

4 Mon numéro de téléphone, c'est le _____

5 J'ai_____ ans.

6 Mon anniversaire, c'est le _____

7 J'ai   _____

8 J'ai les cheveux _____

et les yeux _____

9 Je mesure_____ et je pèse _____ kilos.

> Don't lose marks by missing out bits of information. For example, make sure you write your first name and surname on the ID form as it asks for <u>Prénom et nom de famille</u>.

My world

A Family members

le frère	brother	la sœur	sister
le demi-frère	half-brother	la demi-sœur	half-sister
le beau-frère	step-brother	la belle-sœur	step-sister
le père (papa)	father (dad)	la mère (maman)	mother (mum)
le beau-père	step-father	la belle-mère	step-mother
le grand-père	grandfather	la grand-mère	grandmother
l'oncle	uncle	la tante	aunt
le cousin	cousin (male)	la cousine	cousin (female)
le neveu	nephew	la nièce	niece
le mari	husband	la femme	wife
le fils	son	la fille	daughter

Remember
Beau-frère also means brother-in-law and belle-mère also means mother-in-law.

Q Look back over your classroom work and find key words and phrases to learn from there.

J'ai un frère.	I've got a brother.
Je suis fils/fille unique.	I'm an only child.
J'ai un frère jumeau/une sœur jumelle.	I've got a twin brother/sister.
Mon frère est plus âgé/jeune que moi.	My brother is older/younger than me.
Je suis l'aîné(e).	I'm the eldest.
J'ai une grande famille.	I've got a big family.
J'habite avec mes parents.	I live with my parents.
Mes parents sont divorcés.	My parents are divorced.
Mes parents sont séparés.	My parents are separated.
Mon père s'est remarié.	My father remarried.
Ma sœur m'énerve.	My sister annoys me.
Je m'entends bien avec ma tante.	I get on well with my aunt.

B My friends' characteristics

Remember
If you're talking about a female person, you need to use the adjective endings given here in brackets:
Il est marrant.
Elle est marrante.

marrant(e)	funny	équilibré(e)	even-tempered
intelligent(e)	intelligent	travailleur (travailleuse)	hard-working
patient(e)	patient	poli(e)	polite
calme	quiet	sociable	sociable
content(e)	happy	optimiste	optimistic
impatient(e)	impatient	impoli(e)	impolite
pessimiste	pessimistic	égoïste	selfish
méchant(e)	nasty	idiot(e)/bête	stupid
paresseux (paresseuse)	lazy	timide	shy

un copain/un ami	a male friend
une copine/une amie	a female friend
un voisin/une voisine	a neighbour
un(e) correspondant(e)	a penfriend
Je le/la trouve plein(e) de vie.	I find him/her lively.

My world

C Special occasions

Joyeux Noël!	Happy Christmas!
Joyeuses Pâques!	Happy Easter!
Bonne fête!	Enjoy the holiday!
Bon anniversaire!	Happy birthday!
Bonne année!	Happy New Year!
le Nouvel An	New Year
la fête des Mères/Pères	Mother's/Father's day
le quatorze juillet	14th July (French national day)
la fête	holiday/festival

Remember
In French, you can often use <u>on</u> to talk about what 'one/you/we' do. It follows the same pattern for the verb as <u>il/elle</u> (he/she):
<u>on/il/elle est/joue/danse</u> ...

On chante et danse.	We sing and dance.
On mange des gâteaux.	We eat cakes.
On se fait des cadeaux.	We give presents.
On envoie des cartes de vœux.	We send greetings cards.
On a trois jours de congé.	We have three days off.

C'est un jour en famille.	It's a family day.
C'est une fête religieuse.	It's a religious festival.
C'est une journée spéciale.	It's a special day.
C'est un jour férié.	It's a bank holiday.

Grammar – my, your, his/her etc.

	m. singular	f. singular	plural
	mon oncle	ma tante	ses cousins
	ton père	votre mère	vos enfants
my	mon	ma	mes
your (tu)	ton	ta	tes
his/her	son	sa	ses
our	notre	notre	nos
your (vous)	votre	votre	vos
their	leur	leur	leurs

Q Make a list of six members of your family, for example, John – <u>mon oncle</u>.

PRACTICE

Find the seven family members in this word snake.

ONCLESAMERETWRSEAREFRERESAWSŒURSDPERETANTEASCOUSIN(E)

My world

Family and friends

THE BARE BONES

➤ Make sure you know the key words for members of your family and adjectives to describe their characteristics.

➤ Working out whether sentences are positive, negative, or positive and negative is a popular exam question.

A Yvonne's family

READ

1 Read about Yvonne's family and see if you can underline all the **family members** she mentions.

> Salut. Je m'appelle *Yvonne* et j'habite *La Rochelle*. J'habite avec *ma mère et mon beau-père*. J'ai *une sœur et un demi-frère*. Je m'entends très bien *avec mes parents*, parce qu'ils sont *sympas* et ils *ne sont pas trop strictes*. Mais *mon demi-frère* m'énerve tout le temps – *il a dix ans et il est bête*. Ma *sœur* est *plus* âgée que moi et *elle est équilibrée et intelligente. Elle m'aide à faire mes devoirs et ça c'est formidable!*

2 Now make a list of Yvonne's family members in English, such as 'mother' ...

3 Adapt Yvonne's text above and write about your family. Change the words in *italics* which refer to Yvonne and her family so the text is about you and your family.

Always look and listen out for sentences in the exam you can adapt for your own writing and speaking.

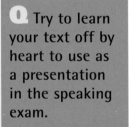

Q Try to learn your text off by heart to use as a presentation in the speaking exam.

B Other people's characteristics

1 Make sure you learn plenty of words for describing people – check the list on page 12 before doing this activity.

WRITE

2 Complétez les phrases. Complete the sentences with suitable adjectives.

Exemple: a Ma mère est jolie, travailleuse et sympa.

a Ma mère/belle-mère est _____

b Mon père/beau-père est _____

c Ma sœur/Mon frère est _____

d Ma meilleure copine est _____

e Mon meilleur copain est _____

Remember
Use words like <u>très</u> (very), <u>vraiment</u> (really), <u>assez</u> (quite) and <u>un peu</u> (a bit) to describe what people are like.

My world

C Positives and negatives

READ

1 In the exam, you might have to say whether statements are positive or negative or sometimes even both positive and negative. Have a go at this activity.

Always read the whole sentence to the end – it might have a positive first half and a negative second half, so don't jump to conclusions too soon.

2 Lisez et écrivez P (positif), N (négatif) ou P+N (positif et négatif). Read and write P (positive), N (negative) or P+N (positive and negative).

a Mon meilleur copain est super marrant. | *P* |

b Notre voisin est pessimiste.

c Mon amie est très impolie envers ses parents.

d Sylvie est intelligente et travailleuse.

e Moi, je suis assez calme mais aussi impatient.

f Mon copain est trop impatient et ça m'énerve.

g Ma correspondante est vraiment méchante.

h Ma copine est paresseuse, mais elle est très sympa.

3 List at least three of your characteristics:
Je suis ...

PRACTICE

What five qualities is this company looking for in its staff?

On recherche des jeunes gens pour travailler dans notre bureau de télécommunications. Vous devez être:

- responsable
- obligeant(e)
- intelligent(e)
- poli(e)
- amical(e)

Lots of French words look like their English meanings, so look out for them in reading tasks like this to make things easier for yourself.

My world

A Rooms

Q Write a list of the rooms in your house.

la cuisine	*kitchen*	la salle à manger	*dining room*
la chambre	*bedroom*	la salle de bains	*bathroom*
le salon/la salle de séjour	*lounge*	le bureau	*study*
le garage	*garage*	les toilettes	*toilet*
la cave	*cellar*		

B Furniture

le fauteuil	*armchair*	la chaise	*chair*
l'armoire/le placard	*cupboard*	le lit	*bed*
la table	*table*	les meubles	*furniture*
la cuisinière à gaz	*gas cooker*	le four	*oven*
le four à micro-ondes	*microwave*	la douche	*shower*
le lavabo	*washbasin*	la machine à laver	*washing machine*
le frigo	*fridge*	le lave-vaisselle	*dishwasher*
la porte	*door*	la fenêtre	*window*
l'escalier	*stairs*	le rideau	*curtain*
le tapis/la moquette	*carpet*	le chauffage central	*central heating*
le mur	*wall*	le miroir	*mirror*

Mes vêtements sont dans l'armoire.	*My clothes are in the cupboard.*
Il y a des disquettes sur la table.	*There are some discs on the table.*
Mes jeux sont sous le lit.	*My games are under the bed.*
Il y a une chaise au pied du lit.	*There's a chair at the end of the bed.*
La télé est au milieu de la chambre.	*The TV is in the middle of the room.*
J'ai des posters partout.	*I've got posters everywhere.*

Q Name all the furniture in your bedroom.

C My house

Remember
You can revise vocabulary all the time at home by naming objects in French you see around you.

J'habite un appartement de (six) pièces.	*I live in a flat with (six) rooms.*
J'habite une maison jumelle.	*I live in a semi-detached house.*
la maison individuelle	*detached house*
le studio	*studio (flat)*
un immeuble	*a block of flats*
Nous avons un grand/petit jardin.	*We've got a big/small garden.*
Nous n'avons pas de pelouse.	*We haven't got a lawn.*
La cuisine se trouve au rez-de-chaussée.	*The kitchen is on the ground floor.*
Il y a trois pièces au premier étage.	*There are three rooms on the first floor.*
J'ai ma propre chambre.	*I've got my own room.*
Je partage ma chambre avec ma sœur.	*I share my room with my sister.*

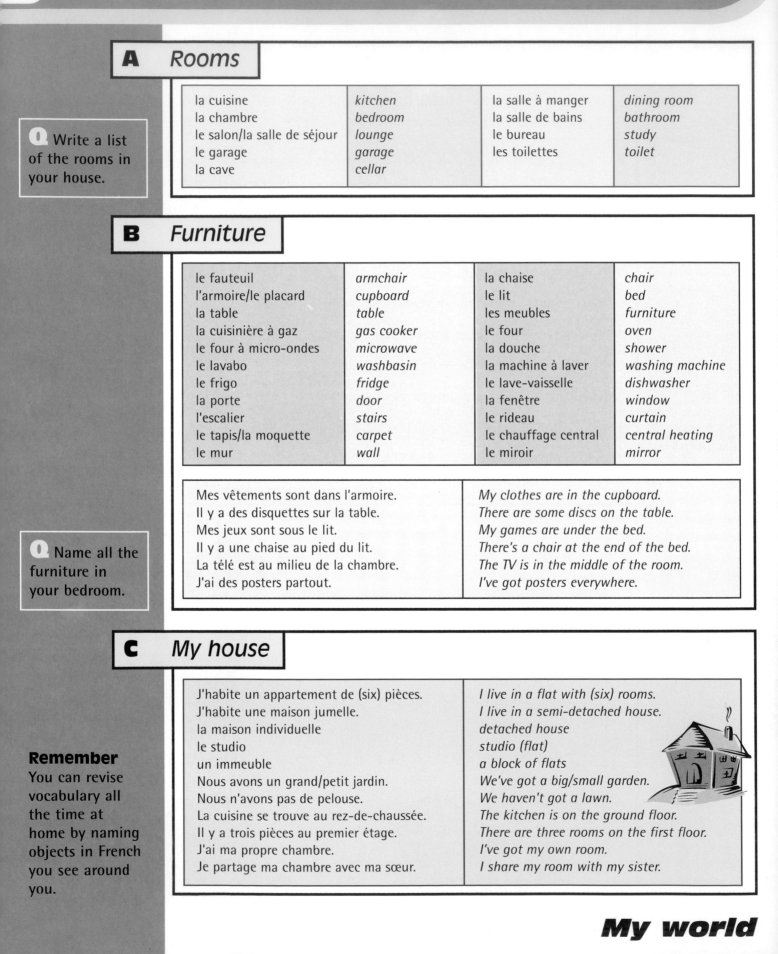

My world

D Location

J'habite/Nous vivons ...	I live/We live ...
dans une ville	in a town
dans un village	in a village
dans la banlieue	in the suburbs
à la campagne	in the country
au bord de la mer	by the sea
sur la côte	on the coast
dans une ferme	on a farm
au centre-ville	in the city centre
dans le sud	in the south
dans le nord	in the north
dans l'ouest	in the west
dans l'est	in the east

Remember
Learn the correct preposition (dans/à etc.) along with the item of vocabulary.

E Further details

Notre bâtiment est ...	Our building is ...
vieux/moderne/laid/beau/grand/petit.	old/modern/ugly/nice/big/small.
Ma ville/La région est ...	My town/The region is ...
historique/industrielle/touristique/belle.	historic/industrial/touristy/pretty.
Il y a beaucoup de bruit ici.	It's very noisy here.
C'est très calme.	It's very quiet.
Il y a mille habitants dans mon village.	There are a thousand inhabitants in my village.
De ma fenêtre, je vois des ...	From my window I can see ...
arbres/fleurs/champs/une rivière.	trees/flowers/fields/a river.

Q Say two sentences about the place you live.

PRACTICE

Say these words out loud in French. Then write them down and check your spellings with the vocabulary opposite. Don't forget to include the word for 'the' each time.

Exemple: a la moquette/le tapis

a carpet

b bed

c curtains

d garden

e semi-detached house

f kitchen

g wall

h shower

i bathroom

j ground floor

My world

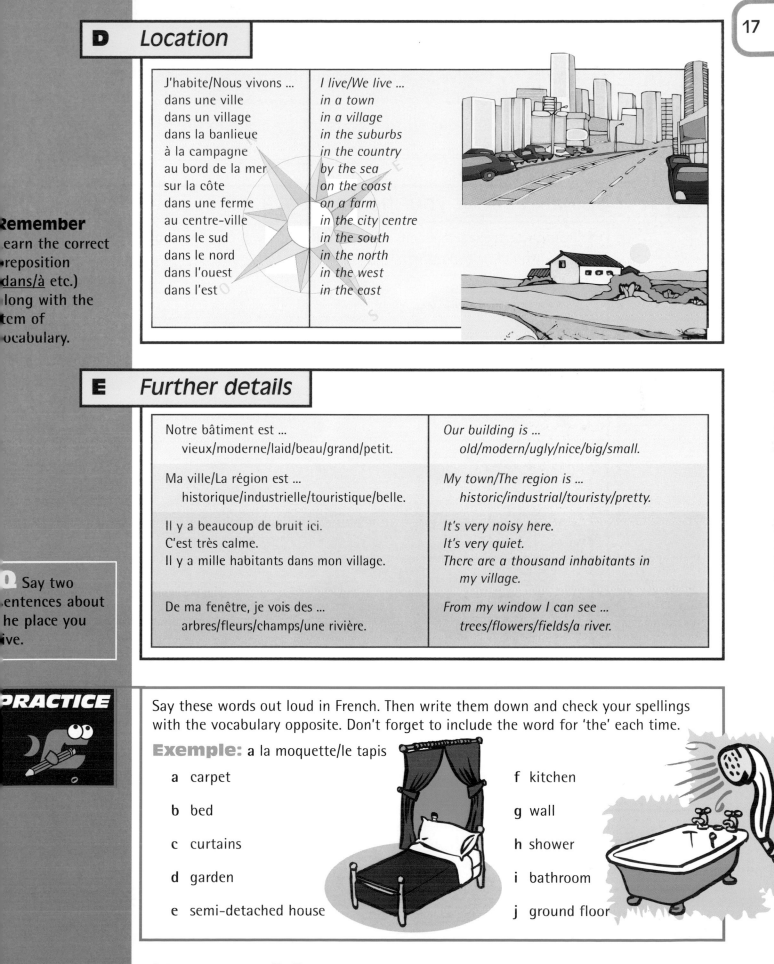

House and home

THE BARE BONES

➤ Always try to give an opinion about the topics you are talking or writing about.

➤ Learn some of your written texts off by heart to use as an oral presentation.

A   Opinions about your home area

READ

Remember
Try to learn whole phrases off by heart, not just single words.

1 Read these teenage opinions and see which ones you could say about your home area. Who likes living where they do?

a J'aime vivre ici parce qu'il y a beaucoup de distractions pour les jeunes.

b J'habite à cinq minutes à pied du centre-ville – et ça c'est pratique.

c Je n'aime pas habiter ici parce que les transports en commun sont terribles, et ça m'énerve.

d J'aime ma ville parce que j'ai beaucoup d'amis qui habitent tout près.

e Je trouve très ennuyeux de vivre ici – le soir il n'y a rien à faire.

h Je déteste habiter dans ce petit village parce que c'est très ennuyeux.

f Dans ma ville, il y a beaucoup de bons magasins, mais par contre il n'y a ni piscine ni centre sportif.

g L'air est pollué à cause des grandes usines.

2 Now **adapt** each sentence so it refers to your home area. For example: speech bubble **a** could easily be turned into: _Je n'aime pas vivre ici parce qu'il n'y a pas de distractions pour les jeunes._

Always try to adapt sentences to make them suit your situation.

Q In speech bubble **g** why is the air polluted?

B My house

READ

1 Read this text through quickly to **get the gist** of what it is about.

> Don't worry about understanding every single word in a text, or translating it word for word – that's just not necessary.

J'habite une maison jumelle dans la banlieue de Nice. Nous avons un petit jardin avec une pelouse et des fleurs. Dans notre maison, il y a une grande cuisine où on prépare et prend les repas. Au rez-de-chaussée, il y a aussi un salon et les toilettes. Ma chambre se trouve au premier étage. C'est une jolie chambre aux murs orange et à la moquette bleue.

Malheureusement, je dois partager ma chambre avec mon petit frère – c'est dommage. Dans la chambre, il y a une table avec un ordinateur, deux lits, une armoire, une chaise et beaucoup de posters. Il y a aussi une chaîne-stéréo et une télévision. Quand mes amis me rendent visite, nous restons souvent dans la chambre et écoutons de la musique, jouons à l'ordinateur et buvons du coca. L'après-midi, je fais toujours mes devoirs dans la chambre.

J'aimerais bien avoir ma propre chambre, mais ça c'est pas possible.
Michel, 16 ans

Q Name five objects Michel has in his room and two things that he does there.

2 Répondez aux questions en français.
Answer the questions in French.

Exemple: a dans la banlieue de Nice

a Où habite Michel?
b Qu'est-ce qu'il y a dans le jardin? (deux choses)
c Où se trouve le salon?
d Comment est la chambre de Michel?
e Avec qui Michel doit partager la chambre?
f Est-ce que Michel peut regarder la télévision dans la chambre?
g Qu'est-ce que Michel et ses amis font dans la chambre? (trois choses)
h Est-ce que Michel est content de partager la chambre avec son frère?

> Don't write full sentences for your answers unless asked to do so. Keep it brief and just give the key information.

Remember
Look out for any questions that have (deux choses) or similar beside them – you'll have to mention the right number of things to get full marks.

PRACTICE

Write a text (80–100 words) about your home and learn it off by heart for a presentation. Write about:

• what sort of a house you live in
• where you live
• what rooms there are in the house
• what your room is like and what is in it
• your opinion on your house

My world

A School subjects

l'informatique	IT	la technologie	technology
les maths	maths	les sciences	science
la biologie	biology	la chimie	chemistry
la géographie	geography	l'histoire	history
l'instruction civique	citizenship	la religion	religion
l'art dramatique	drama	l'éducation physique (EPS)	sport (PE)
le dessin	art	la musique	music

Ma matière préférée, c'est (le français).	My favourite subject is (French).
J'aime bien (l'allemand).	I like (German) a lot.
Je n'aime pas (l'espagnol).	I don't like (Spanish).
Je déteste (la physique).	I hate (physics).
Je suis fort(e) en (allemand).	I'm good at (German).
Je suis nul(le) en (maths).	I'm terrible at (maths).
J'aime (le sport) parce que c'est intéressant/facile.	I like (sport) because it's interesting/easy.
Je n'aime pas (le dessin) parce que c'est difficile/nul.	I don't like (art) because it's difficult/terrible.

Q Can you name four school subjects you like and four you dislike?

B In school

le C.E.S.	comprehensive	le lycée technique	technical college
le lycée mixte	mixed school	le collège privé	private school

le centre sportif	sports centre	la bibliothèque	library
la salle de classe	classroom	le laboratoire	laboratory
la cantine	canteen	la cour	playground

Je vais à (un C.E.S.).	I go to (a comprehensive).
Il y a (un centre sportif).	There's (a sports centre).
Je suis demi-pensionnaire.	I'm a half-boarder (i.e. have school lunches).
Je suis en quatrième/troisième.	I'm in Year 9/10.
Il y a environ mille élèves dans mon collège.	There are about 1000 pupils in my school.
Mon lycée est vieux/grand/moderne.	My school is old/big/modern.
Je porte un uniforme gris et noir.	I wear a grey and black uniform.

Remember Try to remember whether a word is <u>le</u> (masculine) or <u>la</u> (feminine) as you revise vocabulary.

Grammar – 'the' and 'a'

masculine nouns	le = the	un = a	le lycée, le centre sportif
feminine nouns	la = the	une = a	la salle de classe, la cour
nouns beginning a, e, i, o, u, h	l' = the		l'allemand, l'espagnol
plural nouns	les = the		les maths, les sciences

My world

C The 12-hour clock

A dix heures.	At ten o'clock.
Vers six heures.	At about six o'clock.
Il est une heure.	It's one o'clock.
Il est deux/quatre heures.	It's two/four o'clock.
Il est une heure cinq/dix.	It's five/ten past one.
Il est deux heures et quart.	It's quarter past two.
Il est deux heures et demie.	It's half past two.
Il est trois heures moins le quart.	It's quarter to three.
Il est trois heures moins dix/cinq.	It's ten/five to three.
Il est minuit.	It's midnight.
Il est midi.	It's midday.
Quelle heure est-il?	What's the time?

D Daily routine

Je me réveille.	I wake up.
Je me lève.	I get up.
Je me lave.	I wash.
Je m'habille.	I get dressed.
Je prends le petit déjeuner.	I have breakfast.
Je quitte la maison.	I leave the house.
Le premier cours commence.	The first lesson starts.
La récréation est à (dix heures).	Break is at (ten).
Le déjeuner est à (midi).	Lunch is at (twelve).
Les cours finissent à (deux heures).	Lessons finish at (two).
Je fais mes devoirs.	I do my homework.
Le soir, je mange à (huit heures).	I eat at (eight) in the evening.
Je prends un bain.	I have a bath.
Je me couche.	I go to bed.

Grammar – reflexive verbs (se laver/se coucher)

je **me** lave	I wash
tu **te** laves	you wash
il/elle/on **se** lave	he/she/one washes
nous **nous** lavons	we wash
vous **vous** lavez	you wash
ils/elles **se** lavent	they wash
negative: Je **ne** me lave **pas**.	I don't wash.
perfect tense: Je me suis lavé(e).	I washed.

PRACTICE

Copy out the sentences from the daily routine section, adding a time for each one to show when you do them, for example: *Je me réveille à six heures et demie.*

My world

THE BARE BONES

➤ Try to adapt phrases to suit your own situation wherever possible.
➤ Make sure you know how to tell the time in French.
➤ Always give as much detail as you can when asked a question.

A All about school

READ

1 If you have to match sentence halves together or match questions to answers, **always match the ones you're really sure of first**, then have a go at the ones left over.

2 **You don't always need to understand every word of the sentences to match them.** If you see *Quelle est ta matière préférée?* you might be able to work out that *matière* means 'subject' as the question is asking about something you prefer (*préférée*) at school.

3 Faites correspondre. Match the questions with the answers.

1 Quelle est ta matière préférée? **c**

2 Comment est ton prof de français?

3 Comment trouves-tu le français?

4 Quelle matière n'aimes-tu pas?

5 Tu aimes l'histoire?

6 Tu as combien de cours chaque jour?

7 Tu es fort(e) en anglais?

a On a sept cours.

b Non, en anglais je suis nul(le).

c J'aime beaucoup le sport – c'est super.

d Je trouve ça très difficile et compliqué.

e Je déteste la géographie parce que c'est ennuyeux.

f Il est très sympa et amusant.

g Oui, je l'aime beaucoup.

Q Answer the seven questions for yourself, giving as much detail as possible.

B Clocks

SPEAK

1 It's very useful to be able to **say the time properly in French.** You can often add a time in your writing or speaking to make it more interesting.

2 Quelle heure est-il? What's the time?

Exemple: a Il est douze heures et quart.

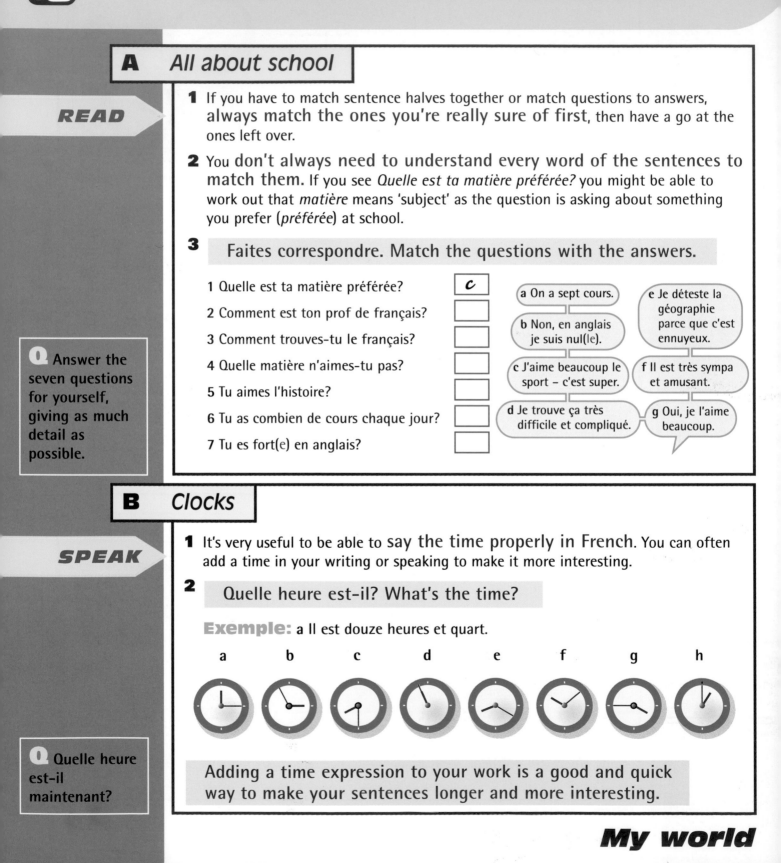

a   b   c   d   e   f   g   h

Q Quelle heure est-il maintenant?

Adding a time expression to your work is a good and quick way to make your sentences longer and more interesting.

My world

Remember

Use <u>ils</u> to refer to mixed genders - masculine and feminine nouns together.

Grammar – pronouns

je	I		nous	we
j'	I (before a, e, i, o, u, h, y)			
tu	you (a friend, relative, child)		vous	you (more than one person, an adult)
il	he		ils	they (masculine/mixed gender plural)
elle	she		elles	they (feminine plural)
on	one/you/we			

C   My school

READ

1 Read this text about Thierry's school and underline all the phrases you think would be useful to write about your school.

> Je suis dans la classe 6T d'un lycée technique. L'école est assez vieille et il y a trente élèves dans ma classe – garçons et filles. Nous passons la plupart de la journée dans notre salle de classe.
>
> Au lycée, il y a aussi des laboratoires et des salles de classe pour faire la musique, le dessin et la technologie. Nous avons une grande bibliothèque où on peut utiliser des ordinateurs ou faire ses devoirs. Le centre sportif est assez grand avec une piscine chauffée, un gymnase et deux terrains de tennis. J'adore aller au centre sportif, parce que je suis très fort en sport.
>
> Le matin, je me lève vers six heures, je me lave et puis je prends le petit déjeuner. A sept heures dix je quitte la maison et je vais à pied au lycée. Le premier cours commence à sept heures et demie et le dernier cours finit vers une heure. Après les cours, je vais à la maison et je fais mes devoirs. Je suis fort en sciences et en maths, mais je trouve l'anglais très difficile et l'histoire un peu ennuyeuse.

Q List four school subjects that Thierry mentions.

2 Answer these questions in English. **Exemple:** a 30

a How many pupils are in Thierry's class?

b What sort of a school does he go to?

c Name three facilities at Thierry's school.

d Why does Thierry enjoy going to the sports centre?

e What time does Thierry leave the house?

PRACTICE

Write a text (80–100 words) about your school and routine and learn it off by heart to say as a presentation. Use the phrases you underlined above to help you. Write about:

- the type and size of school
- the facilities
- your daily routine
- which subjects you are good/bad at

If you have to write about specific details, make sure you write about each detail – cross each one off on the exam paper as you do so.

My world

A Places in town

Remember

Il y a (there is/are) and Il n'y a pas (there is/are not) are useful phrases to learn. Note also that il y a (deux ans) means '(two years) ago'.

un stade	stadium	un aéroport	airport
un monument	monument	un musée	museum
une cathédrale	cathedral	un château	castle
un port	port	une plage	beach
un cinéma	cinema	une église	church
une piscine	swimming pool	un théâtre	theatre
un hôtel de ville	town hall	une mairie	town hall
une gare	station	une gare routière	bus station
un office de tourisme	tourist office	une bibliothèque	library
une université	university	le centre-ville	town centre

Dans ma ville, il y a (un marché).
Il n'y a pas (d'hôpital).

In my town, there's (a market).
There's not (a hospital).

B Shops

une librairie	bookshop	une boutique	small shop
une boucherie	butcher	une parfumerie	perfume shop
une boulangerie	bakery	une pâtisserie	cake shop
une charcuterie	delicatessen	un bureau de tabac	tobacconist
une confiserie	sweet shop	une épicerie	grocery shop
une pharmacie	chemist	un supermarché	supermarket
un grand magasin	department store	un hypermarché	hypermarket
un marché	a market	un centre commercial	shopping centre

Q If you saw a sign saying fermé le mercredi on a shop door, what would it mean?

C'est où, le rayon cadeaux?	Where's the gift department?
L'alimentation est au sous-sol.	Food is in the basement.
C'est au premier étage.	It's on the first floor.
Allez au rez-de-chaussée.	Go to the ground floor.
Où se trouve l'ascenseur?	Where's the lift?
Il faut payer à la caisse.	Pay at the till.
ouvert/fermé	open/closed
heures d'ouverture	opening hours
le vendeur/la vendeuse	sales assistant

C'est où, le rayon cadeaux?

C'est au premier étage.

Holiday time and travel

c Finding the way

Remember
There's nearly always more than one way of saying things. When you're asking the way to places, you can ask:

Comment va-t-on au/à la ...? as well as Où est le/la ...? or Où se trouve le/la ...? or C'est où, le/la ...?

Excusez-moi.	Excuse me.
Pardon?	Pardon
Où sont les toilettes, s'il vous plaît?	Where are the toilets, please?
Où sont les téléphones, s'il vous plaît?	Where are the telephones, please?
Où est l'arrêt d'autobus?	Where's the bus stop?
Où se trouve le cinéma?	Where's the cinema?
Avez-vous un plan de la ville?	Have you got a map of the town?
Avez-vous une carte?	Have you got a map?
C'est à cinquante mètres à droite.	It's fifty metres away on the right.
C'est ici à gauche.	It's here on the left.
Allez tout droit.	Go straight ahead.
Continuez tout droit.	Carry straight on.
Prenez la première rue à droite.	Take the first road on the right.
Prenez la deuxième rue à gauche.	Take the second road on the left.
Traversez le pont.	Cross the bridge.
Traversez la place.	Cross the square.
Allez jusqu'au carrefour.	Go to the crossroads.
Tournez à droite.	Turn right.
au rond-point	at the roundabout
aux feux	at the traffic lights
C'est au coin de la rue.	It's on the corner of the road.
en face de (la gare)	opposite (the station)
entre (la gare) et (la poste)	between (the station) and (the post office)
à côté de (l'hôpital)	next to the (hospital)
près de (la plage)	near to (the beach)
derrière (l'église)	behind (the church)
devant (la banque)	in front of (the bank)
à dix minutes à pied	ten minutes away on foot
à quinze minutes en voiture/vélo	fifteen minutes away by car/bike
Ce n'est pas loin.	It's not far.

Grammar – giving instructions

to a friend (tu)	tourne/traverse/continue/va
to a stranger/adult (vous)	tournez/traversez/continuez/allez
negative	Ne tournez **pas** à droite. Ne traverse **pas** le pont.

PRACTICE

When you're revising French vocabulary, you might find it helpful to draw symbols or sketch pictures for the words to help you remember them.

Draw a picture for each of these phrases to help you learn them.

a tournez à droite

b tournez à gauche

c continuez tout droit

d traversez le pont

e en face de l'église

f à côté de la banque

Holiday time and travel

THE BARE
BONES

➤ Be prepared to come across real French photos in the exam.

➤ If the question says there are four correct sentences to find, keep on looking until you have found the four of them.

➤ Make sure you've learnt your places in town and shops properly.

A Signs

READ

1 Look at the signs below. Can you work out where you'd find each one? How did you work out where they'd be? Which **words and pictures** helped you?

Look carefully at any pictures for some visual help with meaning.

2 In the next activity you are going to match sentences to the signs. **Look for any similarities between the signs and the sentences first.** For example, sign a has **crêperie** and sentence 6 has **crêpes**, and sign c has **cœur de ville** and sentence 4 has **centre-ville**. Are they connected?

Look for similarities wherever possible.

3 C'est quelle photo? Which photo is it?

Q Is the pâtisserie open on Sundays?

Q Which of these places would you go to if you were feeling hungry?

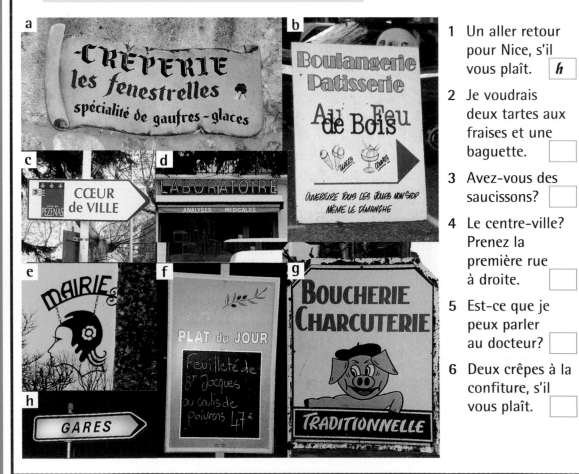

1 Un aller retour pour Nice, s'il vous plaît. **h**

2 Je voudrais deux tartes aux fraises et une baguette. ☐

3 Avez-vous des saucissons? ☐

4 Le centre-ville? Prenez la première rue à droite. ☐

5 Est-ce que je peux parler au docteur? ☐

6 Deux crêpes à la confiture, s'il vous plaît. ☐

Holiday time and travel

B   Shopping centre plan

1 Here, you have to find four correct sentences about a plan – **cross out sentences that are false first** and check to see if four are left over. Then check again that they are all true.

You're only looking for four true sentences here, so the others must be wrong. If you think you've found five true sentences, read them again carefully to find the wrong one.

2   Lisez les phrases et trouvez les quatre phrases vraies.
Read the sentences and find the four true sentences.

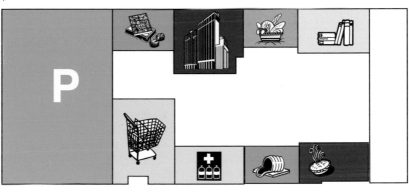

a Le parking est derrière le supermarché.
b Le parking est en face de la pharmacie.
c La pâtisserie est à côté de la boulangerie.
d Il y a un grand magasin entre la confiserie et la boulangerie.
e La confiserie est devant la librairie.
f La boucherie est à côté de la pâtisserie.
g Le supermarché est devant la librairie.
h La pharmacie est en face du grand magasin.

Don't leave a box blank – if you really can't work out the answer, then have a guess at the end of the exam.

Q Est-ce qu'on peut acheter un livre dans ce centre commercial?

Remember
Read small words like <u>entre</u> and <u>devant</u> very carefully – they are important as they tell you about the position of things.

PRACTICE

A friend is visiting you. He's coming by bus. Write directions from the bus stop to your house.

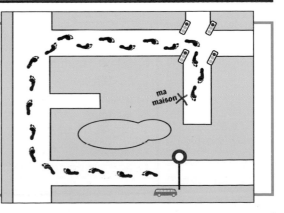

ma maison

Holiday time and travel

A 24-hr clock

Remember
Make sure you know your numbers up to 59 (see page 8) so you can tell the time quickly and easily.

Il est une heure dix.	It's 01:10.
Il est dix heures quinze.	It's 10.15.
Il est treize heures quarante.	It's 13:40.
Il est seize heures vingt.	It's 16:20.
Il est dix-huit heures.	It's 18:00.
Il est vingt-deux heures trente.	It's 22:30.

22:15 SAM

B Buying a train ticket

Remember
Revise asking questions as well as giving answers – you may need to ask questions in the exam.

Un aller simple pour (Calais), s'il vous plaît.	A single ticket to (Calais), please.
Un aller retour pour (Dieppe), s'il vous plaît.	A return to (Dieppe), please.
Première ou deuxième classe?	First or standard class?
Fumeur ou non-fumeur?	Smoking or non-smoking?
Le train est direct?	Is the train direct?
Oui, c'est direct.	Yes, it's direct.
Il faut changer à (Lyon).	You have to change at (Lyon).
C'est le train à destination de (Nice).	The train is going to (Nice).
Le train part de quel quai?	Which platform does the train leave from?
Le train part/arrive à quelle heure?	What time does the train leave/arrive?
A vingt-deux heures dix.	At 22:10.
Est-ce qu'il faut faire une réservation?	Do I have to reserve a seat?
C'est libre?	Is this (seat) free?

TGV   SNCF

C Extras

Q How would you ask for two single tickets to Paris?

composter le ticket (de bus)	to date-stamp the (bus) ticket
acheter un billet/un carnet	to buy a ticket/book of tickets
au guichet	at the counter
le TGV	high-speed train
manquer	to miss
Où est l'entrée?	Where's the entrance?
Le train a du retard.	The train is late.
Défense de fumer dans le train.	No smoking on this train.

Holiday time and travel

D Forms of transport

Je vais à pied.	I go on foot.
Je vais en bus/car.	I go by bus/coach.
Je vais en voiture/taxi.	I go by car/taxi.
Je vais en vélo.	I go by bike.
Je vais en avion/camion.	I go by plane/lorry.
Je vais par le train/métro.	I go by train/underground.

PRACTICE

Look at these words and match them to the signs below.

1 non-fumeur   f
2 compostez le billet
3 les billets
4 la sortie
5 la consigne

6 la salle d'attente
7 les horaires
8 aux voies
9 renseignements

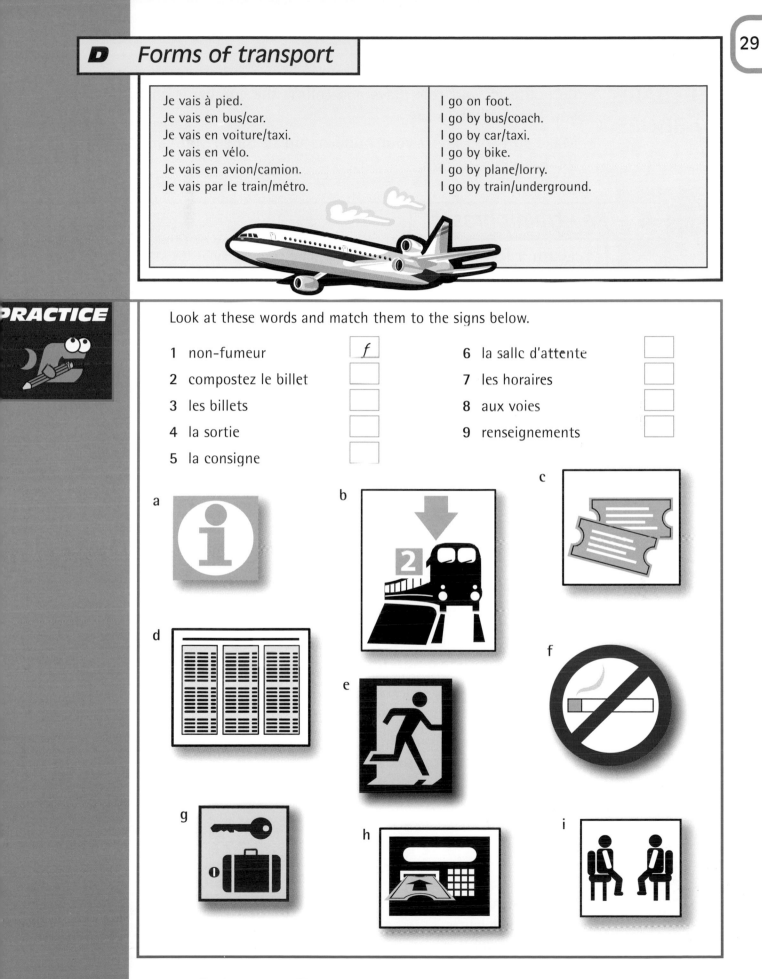

a
b
c
d
e
f
g
h
i

Holiday time and travel

THE BARE
BONES

➤ Be polite in your role plays and follow the cue cards carefully so you know what to say.

➤ Make sure you know your numbers up to 59 so you can say the 24-hour clock times.

A Key train phrases

WRITE

1 Learn a few key phrases in case you get a role play at the station in the exam. Jot down how to ask for these things in French and then check your answers on page 28.

Take care with your spellings, and don't forget any accents (` ´).

a) a single ticket

b) a return ticket to Rouen

c) what time the train leaves

d) a non-smoking seat

e) a first class ticket

f) what time the train arrives

g) which platform it goes from

B Role play – at the train station

SPEAK

1 In the exam you'll probably get symbols rather than word cues for your answers, so make sure you are familiar with them before the exam. **Your teacher will have some examples you can learn from.**

If you don't understand a symbol in the exam, ask the examiner to explain it: <u>Excusez-moi, mais que signifie ce dessin? Je ne le comprends pas</u>.

2 Now have a go at this typical exam role play. The examiner's part is printed below and he/she starts the conversation off.

3 Vous êtes à la gare. Répondez aux questions.
You're at the station. Answer the questions.

1 Bonjour.
2 Vous désirez?
3 Bon, première ou deuxième classe?
4 Pardon?
5 40,69 euros.
6 Dans dix minutes.
   Quai numéro trois.

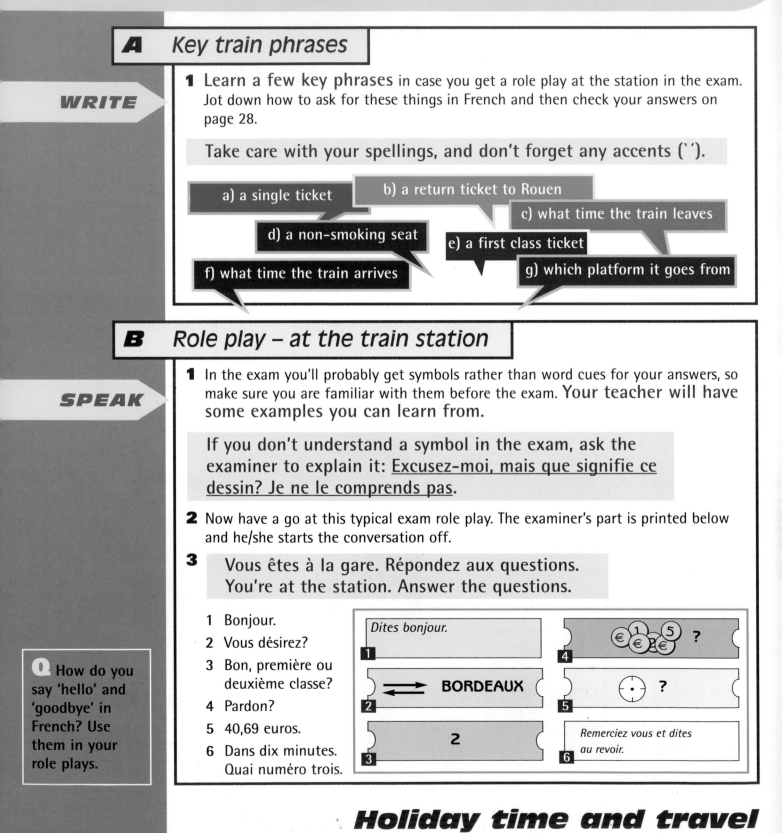

Q How do you say 'hello' and 'goodbye' in French? Use them in your role plays.

Holiday time and travel

C Transport

WRITE

1 Practise writing about forms of transport now. The graph below shows the results of a survey that asked: *Comment allez-vous à votre travail?*

2 Ecrivez les phrases. Write sentences.

Exemple: Dix personnes vont à pied.

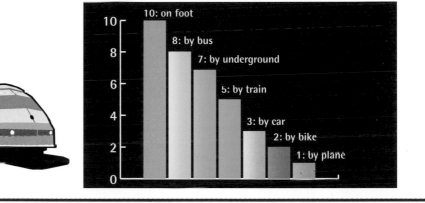

10: on foot
8: by bus
7: by underground
5: by train
3: by car
2: by bike
1: by plane

Grammar – four irregular verbs

	aller (to go)	faire (to do)	vouloir (to want)	pouvoir (to be able to)
je	vais	fais	veux	peux
tu	vas	fais	veux	peux
il/elle/on	va	fait	veut	peut
nous	allons	faisons	voulons	pouvons
vous	allez	faites	voulez	pouvez
ils/elles	vont	font	veulent	peuvent

PRACTICE

Say these times out loud, for example, a would be:
Il est douze heures vingt-quatre.

a 12:24 b 17:30 c 11:16 d 23:45 e 19:35

f 07:05 g 20:51

If you don't understand something in the speaking exam, just ask the examiner: <u>Comment?</u> (pardon?), <u>Je n'ai pas compris</u> (I didn't understand) or <u>Pouvez-vous répéter la question, s'il vous plaît?</u> (Can you repeat the question, please?).

Holiday time and travel

A Countries

Remember
Most countries are feminine, that is <u>la</u>. Exceptions to this include <u>le Canada, le Pays de Galles</u> and <u>le Portugal.</u>

Country	Nationality	
l'Allemagne	allemand(e)	*Germany/German*
les Etats-Unis	américain(e)	*United States/American*
l'Angleterre	anglais(e)	*England/English*
la Belgique	belge	*Belgium/Belgian*
le Canada	canadien(ne)	*Canada/Canadian*
l'Ecosse	écossais(e)	*Scotland/Scottish*
l'Espagne	espagnol(e)	*Spain/Spanish*
la France	français(e)	*France/French*
la Grande-Bretagne	britannique	*Great Britain/British*
la Grèce	grec (grecque)	*Greece/Greek*
la Hollande	hollandais(e)	*Holland/Dutch*
l'Irlande	irlandais(e)	*Ireland/Irish*
l'Italie	italien(ne)	*Italy/Italian*
le Pays de Galles	gallois(e)	*Wales/Welsh*
le Portugal	portugais(e)	*Portugal/Portuguese*
la Suisse	suisse	*Switzerland/Swiss*

le Royaume-Uni	*United Kingdom*
les Pays-Bas	*the Netherlands*
l'Afrique	*Africa*
l'Europe	*Europe*
Douvres	*Dover*
Londres	*London*
Edimbourg	*Edinburgh*

B A past holiday

Remember
When you want to say 'in' you use <u>en</u> with feminine countries and <u>au</u> with masculine ones: <u>en France</u> and <u>au Portugal.</u>

Je suis allé(e) à Nice/à Paris.	*I went to Nice/Paris.*
J'ai voyagé en voiture/en train/en car.	*I went by car/train/coach.*
Je suis allé(e) en avion/en bateau/en bus.	*I went by plane/boat/bus.*
C'était un voyage pénible/formidable.	*It was a dreadful/brilliant journey.*
Je suis resté(e) à la maison.	*I stayed at home.*
J'ai passé une semaine en France.	*I spent a week in France.*
J'ai passé deux jours là-bas.	*I spent two days there.*
J'y étais pendant deux semaines.	*I was there for two weeks.*
L'année dernière, je suis allé(e) à l'étranger.	*I went abroad last year.*
J'ai passé les vacances à la campagne.	*I spent the holidays in the country.*
J'étais sur la côte.	*I was on the coast.*

Holiday time and travel

Je suis allé(e) à la montagne/au bord de la mer.	I went to the mountains/seaside.
Je suis resté(e) dans un camping.	I stayed at a campsite.
Je suis resté(e) chez mes cousins.	I stayed with my cousins.
Il faisait beau/mauvais.	The weather was good/bad.
Je suis allé(e) à la plage tous les jours.	I went to the beach each day.
J'ai nagé dans la piscine.	I swam in the pool.
J'ai visité la cathédrale.	I visited the cathedral.
J'ai acheté des souvenirs.	I bought souvenirs.
Les vacances étaient atroces/magnifiques parce que ...	The holiday was ghastly/brilliant because ...
C'était un pays très ennuyeux/intéressant.	It was a very boring/interesting country.
pendant les vacances d'été/de Pâques	in the summer/Easter holidays
à Noël	at Christmas
quinze jours/un mois	a fortnight/month

Grammar – the perfect tense

participles:

manger →	mangé
finir →	fini
attendre →	attendu

avoir + mangé, fait, voyagé, nagé etc.	or	être + allé(e), resté(e) etc.
j'ai		je suis
tu as		tu es
il/elle/on a		il/elle/on est
nous avons		nous sommes
vous avez		vous êtes
ils/elles ont		ils/elles sont

Remember

If you're using the perfect tense with <u>être</u> verbs, the past participle needs to agree: <u>il est allé, elle est allée, ils sont allés, elles sont allées.</u>

PRACTICE

Look at this luggage label and write a sentence about each country you visited last year, for example, a would be: *Je suis allé(e) en Angleterre.*

a LONDRES
b GENÈVE
c BRUXELLES
d VIENNE
e QUÉBEC
f BRETAGNE
g SÉVILLE
h LISBONNE
i MOSCOU

Holiday time and travel

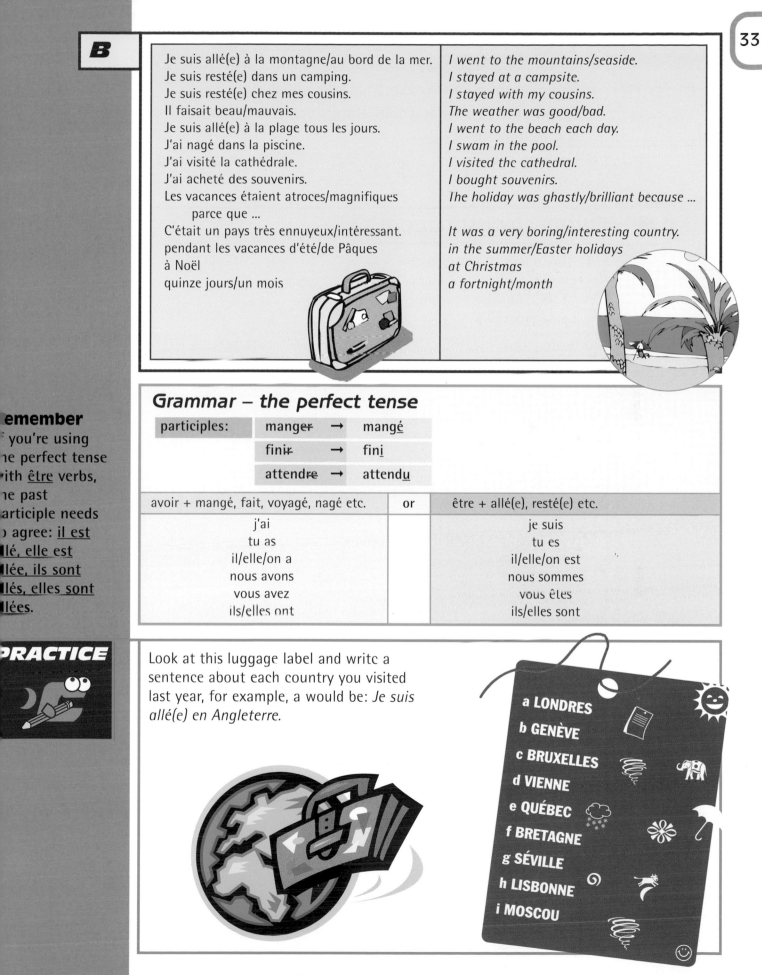

Holiday time

THE BARE BONES

➤ Make sure you know the countries vocabulary.

➤ Be prepared to write about things you have done in the past with the perfect tense.

➤ Use any text in the exam to help you with phrases and vocabulary for your answers.

A European destinations

SPEAK

Q How do you say 'London' in French?

Q Complete this sentence about where you went last summer: <u>L'été dernier, ...</u>

READ

1 Have a look at the map of Europe and see how many of the countries you can name in French.

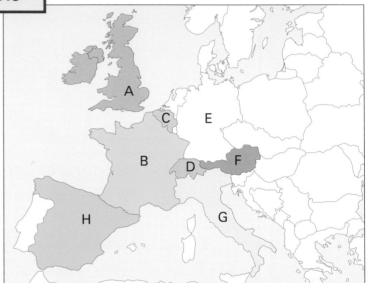

2 Lisez les phrases et trouvez chaque pays sur la carte.
Read these sentences and find each country on the map.

1 Cet été je suis allé en Allemagne. *E*

2 J'ai choisi de rester chez moi en France. ☐

3 Je suis allé en Autriche avec ma famille. ☐

4 En août j'ai voyagé en Espagne. ☐

5 Je suis allé en Grande-Bretagne pendant les vacances. ☐

6 J'ai rendu visité à mes cousins en Suisse. ☐

7 Nous avons passé les vacances d'été en Italie. ☐

8 Mes parents sont allés en Belgique avec ma tante. ☐

Remember
Use <u>être</u> to form the perfect tense of verbs such as <u>aller: je suis allé(e).</u>

Grammar – past participles

avoir	j'ai eu	*I had*	faire	j'ai fait	*I did*
boire	j'ai bu	*I drank*	lire	j'ai lu	*I read*
devoir	j'ai dû	*I had to*	mettre	j'ai mis	*I put on*
dire	j'ai dit	*I said*	pouvoir	j'ai pu	*I could*
écrire	j'ai écrit	*I wrote*	prendre	j'ai pris	*I took*
être	j'ai été	*I was*	voir	j'ai vu	*I saw*
			vouloir	j'ai voulu	*I wanted*

Holiday time and travel

B Holiday adverts

READ

1 Have a look at these three holiday adverts and see if you can work out what they are for exactly.

1
Skiez les 3 vallées
hébergements
de qualité,
de janvier à avril

studio 4 personnes
à 165 euro/semaine

2
Provence
location été
villas de qualité
avec piscine privée

3
Cannes
part.
**loue studio terrasse, vue
mer, terrasse sud**

(fermé tout l'hiver)

Q Which advert is suitable for a February holiday?

2 Now read these sentences from people who stayed in those places. Can you work out who stayed where? In the first example the sentence says they went there in July. You won't necessarily find the word 'July' in the advert – so **look for something which means the same thing**, e.g. 'summer'.

3 Faites correspondre les personnes aux annonces.
Match the people to the adverts.

a   J'y suis allée en juillet.   `2`

b   J'ai nagé dans la piscine.

c   J'ai fait du ski tous les jours.

d   Nous sommes restés dans une villa.

e   J'ai pris le petit déjeuner sur la terrasse.

f   L'année dernière j'ai voyagé en février.

g   Je suis allée dans les montagnes.

h   Je suis allé au bord de la mer.

Q What meal is mentioned in sentences a–h?

PRACTICE

Answer these questions out loud about your (imaginary) last holiday.

Exemple: a J'ai passé les dernières vacances en France.

a   Où avez-vous passé les dernières vacances?

b   Avec qui et comment avez-vous voyagé?

c   Vous y êtes restés combien de temps?

d   Qu'est-ce que vous avez fait?

> Use any questions on the exam paper to help you with your answers. Often you can repeat part of the question with your added-on answer, as in the example here.

Holiday time and travel

A Youth hostel

Remember
Adapt phrases, such as <u>Défense de</u>/<u>Il est interdit de</u>/<u>Vous êtes prié(e)(s) de</u> ... by using another infinitive verb to make further commands: <u>Défense de nager</u> (no swimming), <u>Il est interdit de prendre des drogues</u> (no drug-taking) etc.

une auberge de jeunesse	youth hostel
le lit	bed
le repas de midi/du soir	midday/evening meal
les draps	sheets
la serviette	towel
linge compris	linen included
le dortoir	dormitory
ouvert toute l'année	open all year
adapté(e) pour handicapés	disabled access
la salle de jeux	games room
la salle de réunion	common room
accueil des familles	families welcome
Est-ce que je peux louer (un VTT)?	Can I hire (a mountain bike)?
Je voudrais louer (un bateau).	I'd like to hire (a boat).
Je suis resté(e) dans une auberge	I stayed in a youth hostel.
Il est interdit de manger dans les dortoirs.	No eating in the dormitories.
Défense de fumer dans l'auberge.	No smoking in the hostel.
Vous êtes priés de quitter le bâtiment à dix heures.	Please vacate the building at 10am.
On ferme la porte d'entrée à vingt-trois heures.	The front door is locked at 11pm.
Ne laissez pas vos sacs dans les salles.	Don't leave your bags in the rooms.

B Campsite

Q Cover the vocabulary section and write down five items you would take on a camping trip.

faire du camping	to go camping
le camping	campsite
un emplacement	a site/place (for a tent)
la tente	tent
la caravane	caravan
le sac de couchage	sleeping bag
les allumettes	matches
un ouvre-boîte	tin opener
un canif	penknife
eau potable	drinking water
sale/propre	dirty/clean
Le camping a une piscine/un supermarché/ une laverie.	The campsite has got a pool/supermarket/ launderette.
Ça fait combien?	How much is that?
Est-ce que je dois verser des arrhes?	Do I have to pay a deposit?
J'aime faire du camping.	I enjoy camping.

Holiday time and travel

C *Staying with a penfriend*

Bon voyage!	*Have a good trip!*
Bienvenue.	*Welcome.*
Salut/Bonjour/Au revoir.	*Hi/Hello/Goodbye.*
Bon week-end.	*Have a good weekend.*
Bonsoir/Bonne nuit.	*Good evening/Good night.*
Ça va?	*How are you?*
Ça va bien, merci.	*I'm fine, thanks.*
Ça ne va pas.	*I'm not well.*
J'ai soif/faim.	*I'm thirsty/hungry.*
S'il vous plaît/Merci.	*Please/Thank you.*
De rien.	*Don't mention it.*
Je veux te/vous présenter ma famille.	*I want to introduce you to my family.*
Enchanté(e), Madame/Monsieur.	*Pleased to meet you.*

Je n'ai pas de dentifrice/savon.	*I haven't got any toothpaste/soap.*
Tu as une brosse à dents?	*Have you got a toothbrush?*
Avez-vous une trousse de premiers secours?	*Have you got a first aid kit?*
Je n'ai plus d'argent de poche.	*I haven't got any pocket money left.*

Je te/vous remercie beaucoup.	*Thank you very much.*
Merci de votre hospitalité.	*Thanks for your hospitality.*
Le séjour était agréable/affreux.	*The stay was good/awful.*
C'était une visite agréable.	*It was a nice visit.*
J'étais content(e)/triste.	*I was happy/sad.*

Record words and phrases from the vocabulary sections onto tape. It's often easier to remember words if you say them out loud.

Grammar – past participles with être

je suis allé(e)/arrivé(e)	*I went/arrived*
je suis descendu(e)/monté(e)	*I went down/up*
je suis entré(e)	*I came in/entered*
je suis mort(e)/né(e)	*I died/was born*
je suis parti(e)/resté(e)	*I left/stayed*
je suis rentré(e)/retourné(e)	*I went home/returned*
je suis sorti(e)/venu(e)	*I left/came*
je suis tombé(e)	*I fell*

All reflexive verbs take <u>être</u> too: <u>je me suis lavé(e)</u> = I washed myself.

PRACTICE

Imagine you are at the youth hostel reception desk. Ask to hire these things.

Exemple: a Est-ce que je peux louer des draps?

a   b   c   d

Holiday time and travel

Accommodation

THE BARE BONES

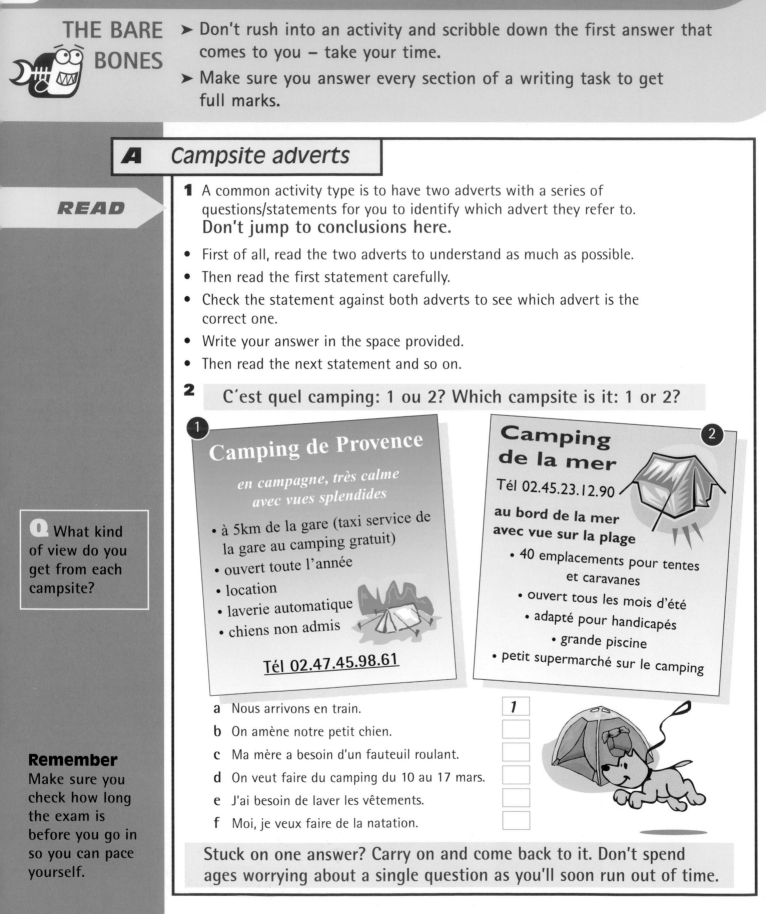

➤ Don't rush into an activity and scribble down the first answer that comes to you – take your time.

➤ Make sure you answer every section of a writing task to get full marks.

A Campsite adverts

READ

1 A common activity type is to have two adverts with a series of questions/statements for you to identify which advert they refer to. **Don't jump to conclusions here.**

- First of all, read the two adverts to understand as much as possible.
- Then read the first statement carefully.
- Check the statement against both adverts to see which advert is the correct one.
- Write your answer in the space provided.
- Then read the next statement and so on.

2

C'est quel camping: 1 ou 2? Which campsite is it: 1 or 2?

1

Camping de Provence

en campagne, très calme avec vues splendides

- à 5km de la gare (taxi service de la gare au camping gratuit)
- ouvert toute l'année
- location
- laverie automatique
- chiens non admis

Tél 02.47.45.98.61

2

Camping de la mer

Tél 02.45.23.12.90

au bord de la mer avec vue sur la plage

- 40 emplacements pour tentes et caravanes
- ouvert tous les mois d'été
- adapté pour handicapés
- grande piscine
- petit supermarché sur le camping

Q What kind of view do you get from each campsite?

a Nous arrivons en train.　　　　**1**

b On amène notre petit chien.

c Ma mère a besoin d'un fauteuil roulant.

d On veut faire du camping du 10 au 17 mars.

e J'ai besoin de laver les vêtements.

f Moi, je veux faire de la natation.

Remember
Make sure you check how long the exam is before you go in so you can pace yourself.

Stuck on one answer? Carry on and come back to it. Don't spend ages worrying about a single question as you'll soon run out of time.

Holiday time and travel

B Visiting a penfriend

READ

1 Read this email through first to **get the gist of it**.

Jean,

Enfin je suis arrivée chez Bethany ici en Angleterre! Le voyage en car était atroce. J'ai quitté la maison à six heures du matin et je suis arrivée à Manchester à sept heures du soir – incroyable, n'est-ce pas? J'étais très fatiguée et aussi un peu triste, mais je me suis couchée de bonne heure et aujourd'hui je me sens bien.

Bethany est très gentille. J'ai oublié beaucoup de choses à la maison (du savon, du dentifrice, mon pyjama et mes pantoufles) mais Bethany m'a prêté tout ça. Ses parents sont aussi très sympas, mais son petit frère est vraiment bête.

Ce matin nous sommes allées dans le centre-ville en train. Manchester est une ville très belle et grande – il y a beaucoup de bruit et des gens partout. C'est super! L'après-midi nous sommes allées regarder un match de foot avec ses parents – non, pas United, mais Manchester City! C'était très ennuyeux mais toute la famille adore le foot, alors ...

Je dois rester encore six jours ici, j'espère que la visite sera un succès et que la France et mes amis ne me manqueront pas trop.

Je dois y aller maintenant – c'est l'heure du dîner.

A bientôt!   Emilie

Q What four things did Emilie leave at home?

2 Now **read the email through in more detail** and **underline the words/phrases** which refer to the pictures below.

3 Lisez et rangez les images dans le bon ordre.
Read and put the pictures in the right order.

| **e** | | | | | |

a   b   c   d   e   f   g

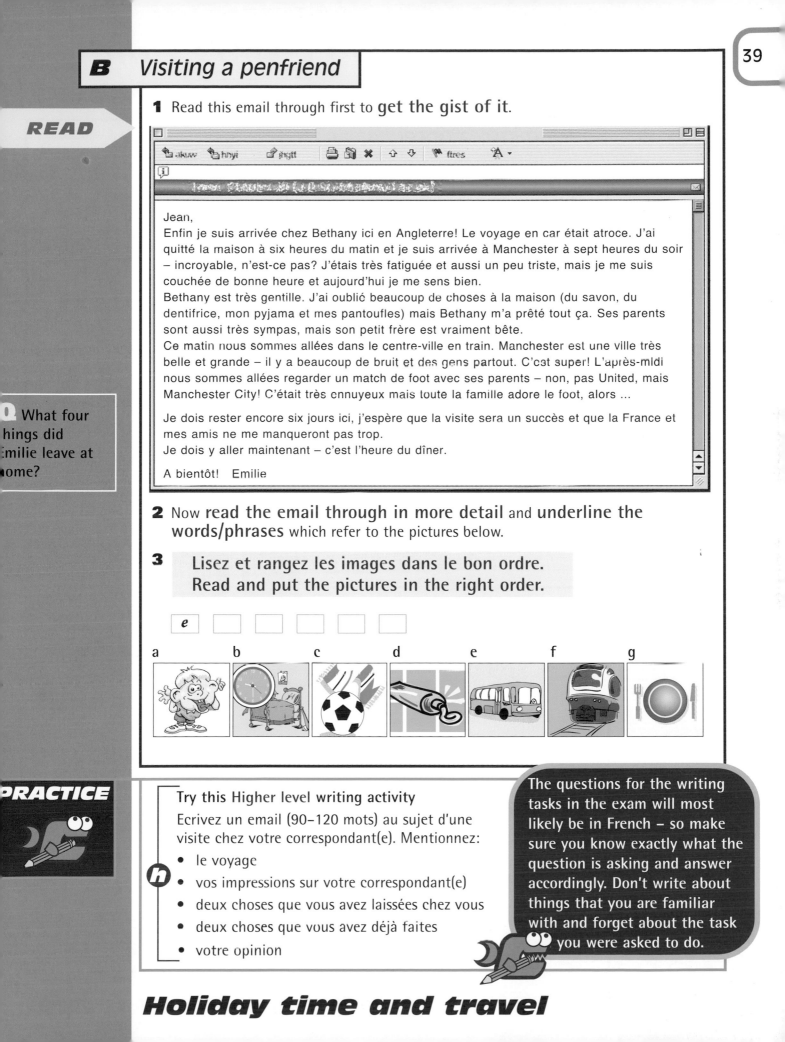

PRACTICE

Try this Higher level writing activity

Ecrivez un email (90–120 mots) au sujet d'une visite chez votre correspondant(e). Mentionnez:

h
- le voyage
- vos impressions sur votre correspondant(e)
- deux choses que vous avez laissées chez vous
- deux choses que vous avez déjà faites
- votre opinion

The questions for the writing tasks in the exam will most likely be in French – so make sure you know exactly what the question is asking and answer accordingly. Don't write about things that you are familiar with and forget about the task you were asked to do.

Holiday time and travel

A Booking into a hotel

Est-ce que je peux vous aider?	Can I help you?
Avez-vous une chambre libre?	Have you got any rooms free?
une chambre pour une personne/deux personnes	a single/double room
Pour combien de personnes?	For how many people?
Vous avez combien d'enfants?	How many children have you got?
Pour combien de nuits?	For how many nights?
Pour deux nuits/personnes.	For two nights/people.
Ça coûte 128 euros par personne par nuit.	That costs 128 euros per person per night.
Avec salle de bains ou douche?	With bath or shower?
Il y a un ascenseur à l'hôtel?	Is there a lift in the hotel?
Il y a un restaurant?	Is there a restaurant?
Pension complète.	Full board.
Demi-pension.	Half board.
Chiens (non) admis.	Dogs (not) permitted.
Payez-vous avec une carte de crédit?	Are you paying by credit card?
C'est à quelle heure, le dîner?	When is dinner?
Où est-ce qu'on peut garer la voiture?	Where can we park the car?

Q How do you ask for a double room?

B Hotel facilities

une salle de jeux	games room
une télévision	television
une douche	shower
les toilettes	toilet
un ascenseur	lift
un restaurant	restaurant
un parking	car park
une vue sur mer	sea view
un balcon	balcony
une piscine	swimming pool
la climatisation	air conditioning

Remember
A good way to learn vocabulary is to make a 'word/picture spider' like the one opposite. Draw pictures or write words, phrases and questions on a topic to help you remember them.

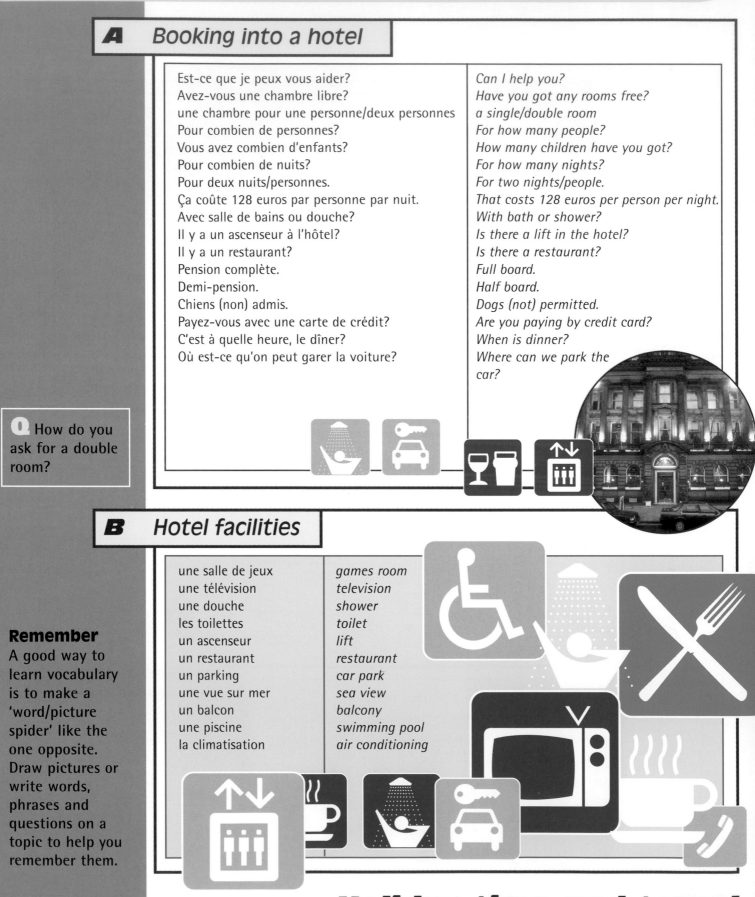

Holiday time and travel

C The weather

Remember
You can pop a weather phrase into your spoken and written work when talking about a variety of topics, e.g. holidays, a special occasion, an outing ...

Quel temps fait-il?	What's the weather like?
Il fait beau.	It's nice.
Il fait chaud.	It's hot.
Il fait froid.	It's cold.
Il y a du brouillard.	It's foggy.
Il fait du soleil.	It's sunny.
Il fait du vent.	It's windy.
Il y a des averses.	There are showers.
Il gèle/neige.	It's freezing/snowing.
Il faisait beau/mauvais.	It was nice/bad.
Il y avait des nuages.	It was cloudy.
Il va pleuvoir.	It's going to rain.
Le climat est pluvieux.	The climate is rainy.
La température sera normale.	The temperature will be normal.
La météo pour demain.	Tomorrow's forecast.

D The seasons

Q Say a sentence about the weather in each season: <u>En été il fait chaud.</u>

le printemps/au printemps	spring/in spring
l'été/en été	summer/in summer
l'automne/en automne	autumn/in autumn
l'hiver/en hiver	winter/in winter

PRACTICE

See how many questions or sentences you can make up by looking at this picture spider.

12.09– 16.09

HOTEL

Exemple:

– Je voudrais une chambre pour une personne.

– Avez-vous des chambres libres?

– Je désire une chambre avec une télévision.

Holiday time and travel

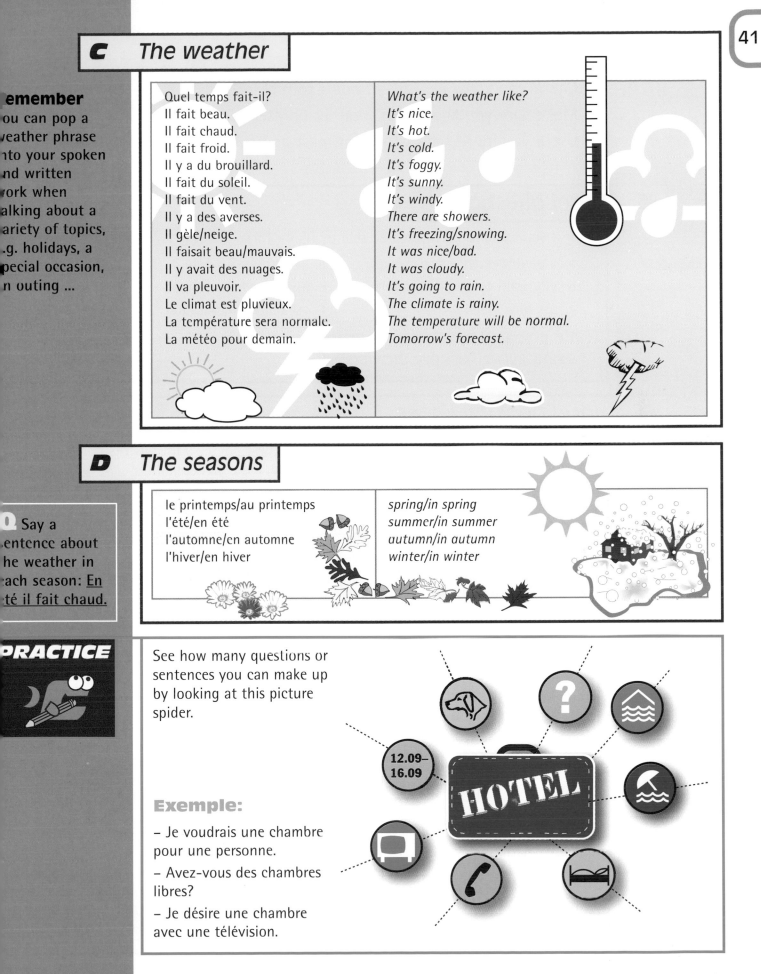

THE BARE BONES

➤ Check you know how to set out a formal letter.
➤ Make sure you know your weather phrases.
➤ Use a variety of tenses (present, past and future) to gain top marks.

A Hotel questions

SPEAK

1 Test yourself and see if you'd be able to ask for these things in an exam role play.

a a double room with a shower

b you want to stay four nights

c ask how much it costs

d ask if there's a pool in the hotel

e ask when breakfast is

f ask one more question

> Be prepared to ask questions in the speaking exam as well as give answers.

B Hotel booking letter

READ

1 Read through this sample letter and underline these points: a the writer's home town and the date, b the address he's writing to, c the greeting, d the sign-off.

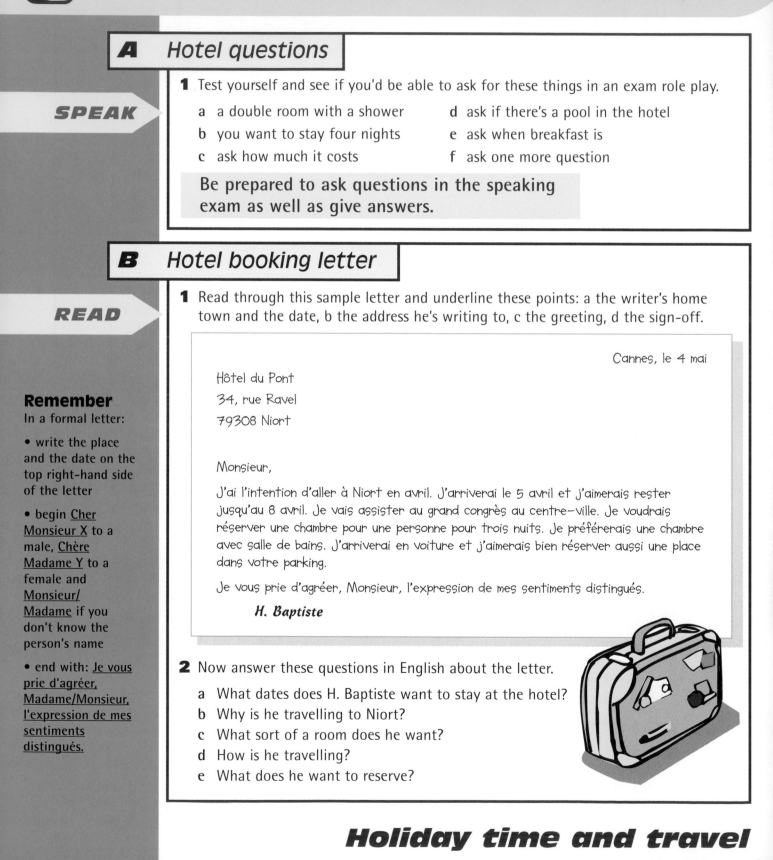

Cannes, le 4 mai

Hôtel du Pont
34, rue Ravel
79308 Niort

Monsieur,

J'ai l'intention d'aller à Niort en avril. J'arriverai le 5 avril et j'aimerais rester jusqu'au 8 avril. Je vais assister au grand congrès au centre-ville. Je voudrais réserver une chambre pour une personne pour trois nuits. Je préférerais une chambre avec salle de bains. J'arriverai en voiture et j'aimerais bien réserver aussi une place dans votre parking.

Je vous prie d'agréer, Monsieur, l'expression de mes sentiments distingués.

H. Baptiste

Remember

In a formal letter:

• write the place and the date on the top right-hand side of the letter

• begin <u>Cher Monsieur X</u> to a male, <u>Chère Madame Y</u> to a female and <u>Monsieur/ Madame</u> if you don't know the person's name

• end with: <u>Je vous prie d'agréer, Madame/Monsieur, l'expression de mes sentiments distingués.</u>

2 Now answer these questions in English about the letter.

a What dates does H. Baptiste want to stay at the hotel?

b Why is he travelling to Niort?

c What sort of a room does he want?

d How is he travelling?

e What does he want to reserve?

Holiday time and travel

C The weather

READ

1 When you do this activity, try and **look for the weather phrase** in each sentence and **ignore the 'padding'** around it. If you don't understand the weather phrase, then use the 'padding' for further help.

2 Lisez les phrases et regardez les images. Où sont les personnes? Read the sentences and look at the pictures. Where is each person?

Exemple: a Bordeaux

a Ici il fait très chaud et je porte un short.

b On est dans les montagnes et on peut faire du ski parce qu'il neige!

c J'attends le bateau et j'ai peur parce qu'il fait du vent.

d Hier j'ai acheté des lunettes de soleil – il faisait du soleil.

e Et moi, je viens d'acheter un parapluie – il pleut tout le temps.

f Hier j'ai pris des photos mais il y avait trop de nuages.

Say the places names out loud – can you pronounce them well in French? (i.e. don't pronounce the final 's' on Paris, Calais or Alpes).

Calais

Paris

Bordeaux 35°C

Strasbourg

Nice

les Alpes

Grammar – faire/avoir/être with weather phrases

today/now	il **fait** beau/du soleil	il y **a** des averses
yesterday/in the past	il **faisait** beau/du soleil	il y **avait** des averses
tomorrow/future	il **fera** beau	il y **aura** des nuages

PRACTICE

Match this Higher level weather forecast to the correct weather map below. Then choose another weather map and write a forecast for it.

Le temps sera nuageux et humide sur une bonne moitié nord-ouest du pays où le vent se lèvera. Des pluies ou des averses parfois orageuses pourront se produire, surtout sur les régions du sud et de l'est. Ailleurs il fera encore assez beau mais le ciel tendra à se voiler. Il fera un peu frais le matin mais doux en journée.

mercredi   jeudi   vendredi   samedi

Be prepared to come across present, past and future tenses in the reading exam.

Holiday time and travel

A Telephone

Q What is your phone code and number? Say them out loud in French.

C'est X à l'appareil.	It's X on the phone.
Allô, Christophe?	Hello, is that Christophe?
Est-ce que je peux parler à X?	Can I talk to X?
Je suis désolé(e), mais … n'est pas là.	I'm sorry, but … isn't here.
Je peux laisser un message?	Can I leave a message?
Je rappellerai plus tard.	I'll ring back later.
Quel est votre numéro de téléphone?	What's your phone number?
C'est le zéro un, dix, vingt, douze, quarante-cinq.	01.10.20.12.45
C'est quoi, l'indicatif?	What's the code?

B Bank

Remember
The French currency is the euro. A hundred cents make up one euro. You'll also come across the old currency, the franc, in your reading. There were a hundred centimes to the franc.

Je cherche une banque.	I'm looking for a bank.
Où se trouve le bureau de change?	Where's the bureau de change?
Je voudrais changer un chèque de voyage.	I'd like to change a traveller's cheque.
Je dois changer des livres sterling en euros.	I need to change pounds sterling to euros.
La livre est à combien?	What rate is the pound?
Elle est à 1 euro 56.	It's 1 euro 56.
Il faut payer une commission.	You have to pay commission.
Allez à la caisse.	Go to the counter.
un billet de 50 euros	a 50 euro note
une pièce de 50 centimes	a 50 centime coin
la monnaie	currency, change

C Post

Je vais à la poste.	I'm going to the post office.
Où se trouve la boîte aux lettres?	Where's the letter box?
Je voudrais envoyer une lettre en France.	I'd like to send a letter to France.
Je voudrais trois timbres à deux euros.	I'd like three two-euro stamps.
Quatre timbres pour l'Angleterre, s'il vous plaît.	Four stamps for England, please.
la lettre	letter
la carte postale	postcard
le paquet	packet

Q How would you ask for six 50-cent stamps?

Holiday time and travel

D Reporting a loss

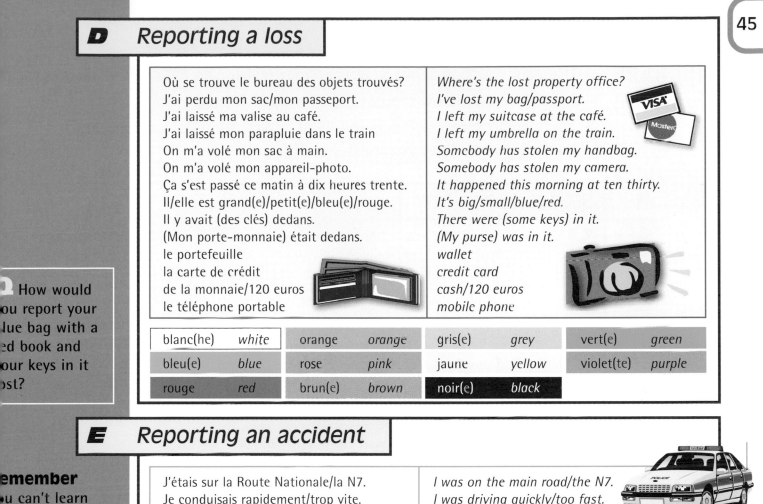

Où se trouve le bureau des objets trouvés?	Where's the lost property office?
J'ai perdu mon sac/mon passeport.	I've lost my bag/passport.
J'ai laissé ma valise au café.	I left my suitcase at the café.
J'ai laissé mon parapluie dans le train	I left my umbrella on the train.
On m'a volé mon sac à main.	Somebody has stolen my handbag.
On m'a volé mon appareil-photo.	Somebody has stolen my camera.
Ça s'est passé ce matin à dix heures trente.	It happened this morning at ten thirty.
Il/elle est grand(e)/petit(e)/bleu(e)/rouge.	It's big/small/blue/red.
Il y avait (des clés) dedans.	There were (some keys) in it.
(Mon porte-monnaie) était dedans.	(My purse) was in it.
le portefeuille	wallet
la carte de crédit	credit card
de la monnaie/120 euros	cash/120 euros
le téléphone portable	mobile phone

blanc(he)	*white*	orange	*orange*	gris(e)	*grey*	vert(e)	*green*
bleu(e)	*blue*	rose	*pink*	jaune	*yellow*	violet(te)	*purple*
rouge	*red*	brun(e)	*brown*	noir(e)	*black*		

How would you report your blue bag with a red book and your keys in it lost?

E Reporting an accident

Remember
You can't learn ALL the vocabulary in this book off by heart but aim to look each section you'll be able recognise a lot vocabulary in the exam.

J'étais sur la Route Nationale/la N7.	I was on the main road/the N7.
Je conduisais rapidement/trop vite.	I was driving quickly/too fast.
Je n'ai pas vu le feu rouge.	I didn't see the red light.
L'accident s'est passé sur l'autoroute A6.	The accident happened on the A6 motorway.
Police-secours est arrivée à toute vitesse.	The emergency services arrived at top speed.
Une ambulance est arrivée.	An ambulance arrived.
Le gendarme a noté les détails.	The policeman noted the details.
Il ne portait pas de ceinture de sécurité.	He wasn't wearing a seatbelt.
J'ai appelé police-secours.	I called 999.
Je suis allé(e) à l'hôpital.	I went to hospital.
Il y avait deux morts.	Two people were killed.
Je n'étais pas blessé(e).	I wasn't injured.
Au secours!	Help!

PRACTICE

Fill in the missing words from the box below.
- (a) .... C'est combien pour envoyer une lettre et (b) .... en Italie?
- Ça fait 45 (c) .... pour une carte postale ou (d) ....
- Alors, six (e) .... à 45 cents, s'il vous plaît.
- Voilà. C'est (f) ....?
- Non, je voudrais envoyer ce (g) .... en Australie.
- Bon, il faut le peser . . . ça fait 13 euros 60.
- Merci bien, c'est tout.
- Alors, ça fait 16 (h) .... 30.
- Voilà.
- Au revoir, madame.
- (i) ....

Au revoir	paquet
timbres	cents
	une carte postale
Bonjour	une lettre
euros	tout

Holiday time and travel

Public services

THE BARE BONES
➤ Use your common sense as well as your revision to help you in the exam.
➤ Make sure you know the question words in French.
➤ You'll come across numbers in lots of topics, so make sure you are confident with them (pages 8 and 65).

A Using a phone box

READ

1 Read these phone box instructions to see if you can work out what they mean. Use your **common sense** when doing activities like this one. If you don't know what *décrochez* and *raccrochez* mean, just think for a moment:

- they are probably related words as they are very similar, both with *crochez* at the end
- what are you likely to do both after going into a phone box and before leaving? (Pick up and put down the receiver.)

Similarly, you should be able to work out that a *télécarte* is a phone card, even though you may never have met the word before.

> A bit of common sense will help you in your exams.

2 **Faites correspondre les phrases 1–9 aux images a–i.**
Match the sentences 1–9 to the correct pictures a–i.

1 Entrez dans la cabine téléphonique. `f`
2 Décrochez.
3 Introduisez la télécarte.
4 Attendez la tonalité.
5 Composez le numéro.
6 Parlez.
7 Raccrochez.
8 Retirez la télécarte.
9 Quittez la cabine téléphonique.

Q Can you change these instructions to the tu form? For example entrez becomes entre.

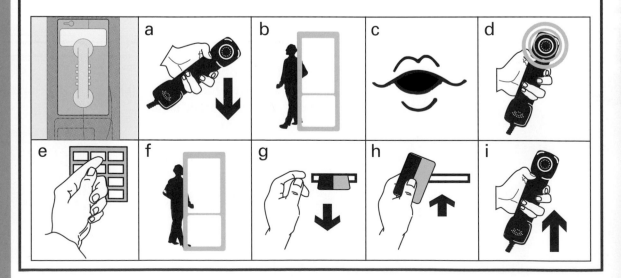

Holiday time and travel

B Lost and found

WRITE

1 See if you can **identify these pictures** and so guess at the words you will be looking out for in the notices below. Try to identify the colours or any details as well and jot down words you might expect to find.

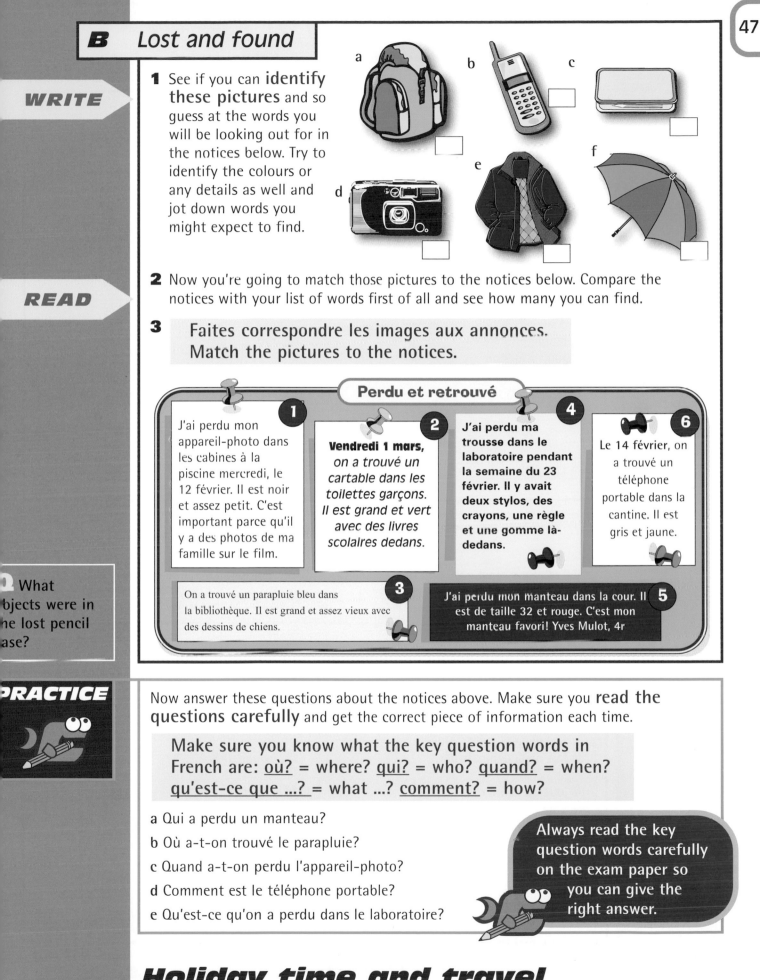

a
b
c
d
e
f

READ

2 Now you're going to match those pictures to the notices below. Compare the notices with your list of words first of all and see how many you can find.

3 Faites correspondre les images aux annonces.
Match the pictures to the notices.

Perdu et retrouvé

1 J'ai perdu mon appareil-photo dans les cabines à la piscine mercredi, le 12 février. Il est noir et assez petit. C'est important parce qu'il y a des photos de ma famille sur le film.

2 **Vendredi 1 mars,** on a trouvé un cartable dans les toilettes garçons. Il est grand et vert avec des livres scolaires dedans.

4 J'ai perdu ma trousse dans le laboratoire pendant la semaine du 23 février. Il y avait deux stylos, des crayons, une règle et une gomme là-dedans.

6 Le 14 février, on a trouvé un téléphone portable dans la cantine. Il est gris et jaune.

3 On a trouvé un parapluie bleu dans la bibliothèque. Il est grand et assez vieux avec des dessins de chiens.

5 J'ai perdu mon manteau dans la cour. Il est de taille 32 et rouge. C'est mon manteau favori! Yves Mulot, 4r

Q What objects were in the lost pencil case?

PRACTICE

Now answer these questions about the notices above. Make sure you **read the questions carefully** and get the correct piece of information each time.

Make sure you know what the key question words in French are: **où?** = where? **qui?** = who? **quand?** = when? **qu'est-ce que ...?** = what ...? **comment?** = how?

a Qui a perdu un manteau?

b Où a-t-on trouvé le parapluie?

c Quand a-t-on perdu l'appareil-photo?

d Comment est le téléphone portable?

e Qu'est-ce qu'on a perdu dans le laboratoire?

Always read the key question words carefully on the exam paper so you can give the right answer.

Holiday time and travel

A Hobbies

jouer aux cartes	*to play cards*
lire	*to read*
nager	*to swim*
faire du sport	*to do sport*
faire du théâtre	*to do acting*
écouter de la musique	*to listen to music*
regarder la télé	*to watch TV*
jouer du violon/piano	*to play the violin/piano*
jouer aux jeux électroniques	*to play electronic games*
aller au cinéma	*to go to the cinema*
aller au concert/club	*to go to a concert/club*
faire une promenade	*to go for a walk*
retrouver mes amis/amies	*to meet my friends*
aller à la maison des jeunes	*to go to the youth club*
faire de la cuisine	*to cook*

J'aime/J'adore (nager).	*I like/love (swimming).*
Je déteste/Je n'aime pas (lire).	*I hate/dislike (reading).*

Remember

The verbs <u>aimer</u>, <u>adorer</u>, <u>détester</u> and <u>vouloir</u> are followed directly by the infinitive without any prepositions, e.g. <u>j'aime danser</u>.

Remember

Carry this book with you wherever you go, so that you can test yourself on French words and phrases.

Grammar – verbs with an infinitive

j'adore/j'aime	*(I love/like)*	nager, danser, lire
je déteste/je n'aime pas	*(I hate/dislike)*	jouer aux cartes, regarder la télé
je voudrais	*(I'd like to)*	aller an cinéma, faire du sport

B Sports

Je fais du vélo/cyclisme.	*I go cycling.*
Je fais du cheval/de l'équitation.	*I go horseriding.*
Je fais de la natation.	*I go swimming.*
Je fais de la planche à voile.	*I go windsurfing.*
Je fais de la gymnastique.	*I do gymnastics.*
Je joue au football.	*I play football.*
Je joue au tennis.	*I play tennis.*
Je joue au basket/volley.	*I play basketball/volleyball.*
Je vais à la pêche.	*I go fishing.*
J'aime courir.	*I like running.*
Je trouve ça fatigant.	*I find that tiring.*
Mon sport préféré, c'est (la natation).	*My favourite sport is (swimming).*

Q Write a list of eight sports you might do on an activity holiday.

C How often?

lundi	(on) Monday	vendredi	(on) Friday
mardi	(on) Tuesday	samedi	(on) Saturday
mercredi	(on) Wednesday	dimanche	(on) Sunday
jeudi	(on) Thursday	le week-end	at the weekend

le lundi/le samedi	on Mondays/Saturdays
(Je fais ça) le soir.	(I do that) in the evenings.
tous les jours	every day
souvent	often
chaque week-end	each weekend
de temps en temps	now and again
L'hiver, (je fais du ski).	(I go skiing) in the winter.
Je m'entraîne (chaque week-end).	I train (each weekend).
Je suis sportif (sportive).	I'm sporty.
Je ne suis pas sportif (sportive).	I'm not sporty.

Remember

Ask a friend or a member of your family to help you learn vocabulary by testing you or learning with you.

PRACTICE

Remember

Check your written answers to the activities in this book in the answer section or ask your teacher to make sure you are getting your spellings right.

Fill in the gaps to label the photos.

a du _ _ _ k _ _

b du _ _ _ o

c du _ k _

d du f _ _ _ _ _ _ _

e du _e_ _i_ de _ _ _ _ e

f de la _ _ t _ _ _ _ n

g de la v _ _ _ _

h du t _ _ _ _ _

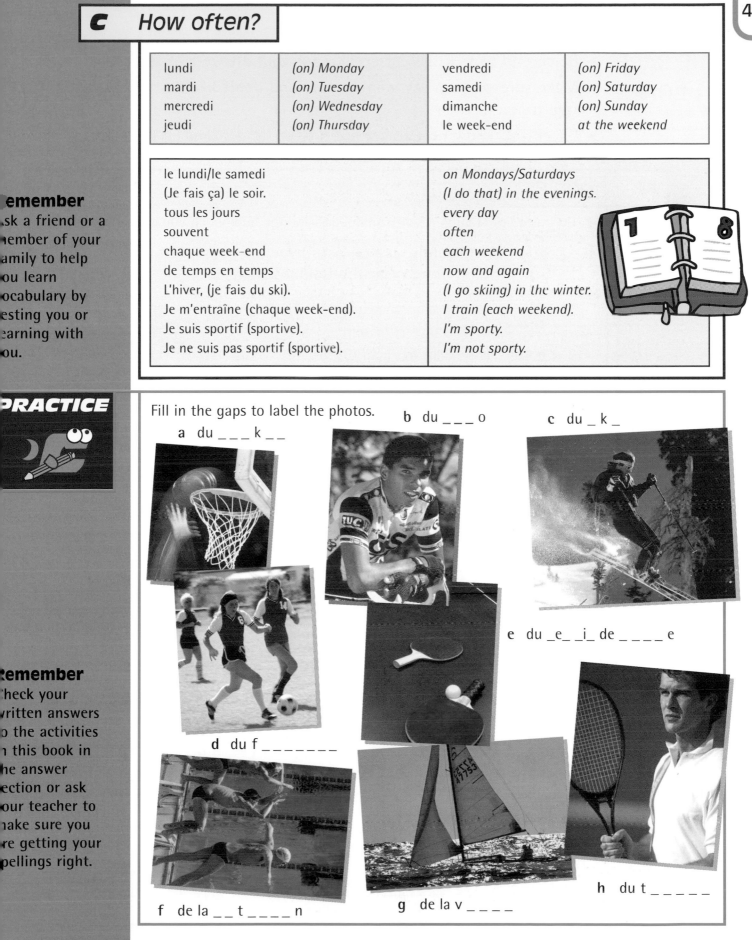

Work and lifestyle

Free time

➤ Be careful to tick the correct box for your answers in the exam.

➤ Make sure you can say what you do and don't like doing in your free time.

➤ Check you know how to set out a letter to a friend in French.

A Hobbies

READ

1 Do this quick reading activity on hobbies and see how much you can understand.

2 **Faites correspondre les phrases avec les passe-temps. Match the sentences to the hobbies.**

1 Il y a onze joueurs dans une équipe. On le joue à Elland Road et Old Trafford par exemple.

2 C'est un passe-temps très actif! On écoute de la musique. On le fait souvent à la disco.

3 On regarde beaucoup de films.

4 C'est un passe-temps très paresseux – on est dans le salon ou dans sa chambre et on regarde un écran.

5 Pour ce passe-temps il faut peut-être aller à la bibliothèque.

a lire
b jouer au football
c regarder la télé
d danser
e aller au cinéma

Q Which hobby a–e does this person like: J'aime aller aux boums?

B Giving detailed answers about hobbies

1 If someone asks you: *Quel est ton passe-temps préféré?* you could reply:

a Ecouter de la musique.

SPEAK

b J'aime bien écouter de la musique.

c J'adore écouter de la musique – surtout les disques de Britney.

2 **Which answer above do you think is more interesting?** Well, it has to be answer c because it contains **the most information.**

3 Answer the questions on page 51 with as much detail as possible. The phrases in the vocabulary section on pages 48–49 will help you, as will the suggestions opposite.

Exemple:

a J'aime bien jouer au rugby et regarder la télé. Le rugby – c'est formidable et j'y joue chaque week-end. Je regarde souvent la télé parce que j'ai une télé dans ma chambre. J'adore les feuilletons et les films d'aventure, mais je n'aime pas les documentaires sur les animaux – ils ne m'intéressent pas du tout.

Work and lifestyle

B

Remember
Try and add a reason by each statement with <u>parce que</u> (because) or add another activity with <u>et</u> (and).

a Quel est ton passe-temps préféré?
J'aime/J'adore ...

> going to the cinema/love action films in particular/but it's expensive

b Qu'est-ce que tu aimes faire le week-end?
J'aime/J'adore ...

> meeting my friends/that's fun/we go to town and go shopping on Saturday and we play football on Sunday

c Qu'est-ce que tu n'aimes pas faire dans ton temps libre?
Je n'aime pas/Je déteste ...

> doing my homework/boring and often difficult

C Sports

READ

1 Make sure you **tick the correct box** each time in this activity. Don't lose out on marks by accidentally crossing a box you don't mean to.

Tick the ones you are sure of first and then go back and fill in any blanks.

2 Sportif ou non? Are these people sporty or not?

		sportif	non
a	L'hiver, je fais du ski.	✔	
b	Je déteste faire du hockey sur glace		
c	J'adore faire du patin à roulettes – c'est formidable!		
d	Le samedi, je joue au base-ball au centre sportif.		
e	Je n'aime pas jouer au foot – j'ai toujours froid.		
f	Le rugby c'est un sport terrible – je déteste ça.		
g	De temps en temps je fais de l'escalade parce que mon père en fait.		
h	J'aime courir et jouer au tennis, mais je déteste nager.		

Q List six sports in English that are mentioned here.

PRACTICE

Read this letter and write a reply (40 words) to Georges.
Answer his question with as much detail as possible.

Dieppe, le 4 mai

Chère Sylvie,

Aujourd'hui je t'écris au sujet des passe-temps! Moi, j'aime bien aller au cinéma avec mes copains. J'aime aussi jouer au tennis le week-end. Quels sont tes passe-temps préférés?

A bientôt
Georges

Follow the layout of any example letter – your town and date go on the top right-hand side and you start with <u>Cher</u> for a boy and <u>Chère</u> for a girl. Finish your letter in the same way: <u>A bientôt!</u>

Work and lifestyle

Media – vocabulary

A Television

les documentaires	documentaries
les informations/les actualités	the news
les feuilletons	serials/soap operas
les dessins animés	cartoons
les émissions de sport	sports programmes
les émissions de musique	music programmes
Je regarde la télévision tous les jours/soirs.	I watch television every day/evening.
Mon émission préférée, c'est «Les Simpson».	My favourite programme is 'The Simpsons'.
J'aime bien (les films).	I like (films).
Je n'aime pas (les jeux télévisés).	I dislike (game shows).
J'aime regarder (le sport).	I like watching (sport).

B Music

Remember
Many French words look like their English equivalents – look at these phrases and see!

Mon chanteur préféré, c'est X.	My favourite male singer is X.
Ma chanteuse préférée, c'est X.	My favourite female singer is X.
Ma chanson préférée, c'est X.	My favourite song is X.
Mon groupe préféré, c'est X.	My favourite group is X.
la musique pop/rock/classique	pop/rock/classical music
J'aime écouter la radio.	I like listening to the radio.
J'achète des CDs/cassettes.	I buy CDs/cassettes.

C Cinema

On passe un film d'amour.	There's a love film on.
J'adore (les films comiques).	I love (comedies).
Je déteste (les films d'épouvante).	I hate (horror films).
un film d'aventure/d'horreur	adventure/horror film
un film de science-fiction	science fiction film
la vedette de cinéma	film star
être célèbre/important(e)	to be famous/important

D Theatre

Remember
Try to use some past tense phrases in your work – c'était (it was) is an easy way of doing so.

J'adore aller au théâtre.	I love going to the theatre.
Les acteurs étaient excellents.	The actors were great.
L'actrice principale était nulle.	The main actress was dreadful.
La musique était formidable.	The music was great.
C'était une bonne soirée.	It was a good evening.
Je n'avais pas une bonne place au balcon.	I didn't have a good seat in the balcony.
C'était une pièce intéressante/ennuyeuse.	It was an interesting/boring play.
un acteur/une actrice	actor/actress

Work and lifestyle

Grammar – imperfect tense (avoir/être)

avoir	être
j'avais (I had)	j'étais (I was)
tu avais	tu étais
il/elle/on avait	il/elle/on était
nous avions	nous étions
vous aviez	vous étiez
ils/elles avaient	ils/elles étaient

E Books

L'histoire n'était pas bonne.	The story wasn't good.
Il s'agissait d'une famille.	It was about a family.
Ça se passait en Italie.	It took place in Italy.
C'était triste/amusant.	It was sad/funny.
J'ai beaucoup pleuré/ri.	I cried/laughed a lot.
Je l'ai trouvé compliqué.	I found it complicated.
C'était comique/drôle/amusant.	It was comic/funny.
J'aime lire les romans.	I like reading novels.
Je lis le journal chaque jour.	I read the paper every day.
Récemment j'ai lu un livre de science-fiction.	I read a science fiction book recently.
C'était un roman compliqué/difficile.	It was a complicated/difficult novel.
J'adore les bandes dessinées.	I love comics.
un écrivain bien connu	a well-known writer

Remember A lot of these expressions can be used when talking about films, plays and television programmes.

F Inviting somebody out

Tu es libre ce week-end?	Are you free this weekend?
Si on allait au cirque?	Shall we go to the circus?
On va au spectacle/au match?	Shall we go to a show/match?
Tu veux aller à la discothèque?	Do you want to go to a disco?
Tu veux faire une excursion?	Do you want to go on a trip?
J'accepte ton invitation.	I accept your invitation.
Oui, d'accord. Je veux bien.	Yes, I'd love to.
Ça ne me dit rien.	I don't fancy that.
Je regrette/Je suis désolé(e) mais je ne suis pas libre.	I'm sorry but I'm not free.
On se retrouve à quelle heure?	When shall we meet?
On se retrouve à six heures.	We'll meet at six o'clock.
On se retrouve où?	Where shall we meet?

On se retrouve chez moi/à la gare/à l'école.	We can meet at my house/the station/school.
Ça coûte combien l'entrée?	How much is the entrance fee?

Remember Say five French words or three phrases out loud every morning before you get out of bed.

PRACTICE

Make up a little dialogue to invite a friend to the cinema on Saturday night.

Exemple: Jean, tu es libre ce samedi soir?

Work and lifestyle

THE BARE BONES

➤ Try to get your French pronunciation sounding really good by practising out loud whenever possible.

➤ Learn plenty of vocabulary about films and TV programmes before the exam to make it easier for yourself.

A   TV and music questionnaire

READ

1 In this activity, you are going to tick the correct answer to provide information about your watching/listening preferences.

> Always read all the possible answers before you tick a box on multiple choice questions.

Remember
Look up any words you don't know in a dictionary, or ask your teacher – make a note of them in your vocabulary book to learn.

2   Complétez le sondage. Complete the survey.

1 Je regarde la télé en moyenne:
a) plus de 3 heures par jour ☐
b) 1–3 heures par jour ☐
c) moins d'une heure par jour ☐

2 Chez nous, on a:
a) une télé dans le salon ☐
b) une télé dans le salon et une télé dans ma chambre ☐
c) plus de deux télés ☐

3 Mes parents interdisent la télé:
a) tout le temps ☐
b) après dix heures le soir ☐
c) de temps en temps ☐

4 J'aime surtout regarder:
a) le sport ☐
b) les feuilletons ☐
c) les séries policières ☐

5 Je n'aime pas regarder:
a) le sport ☐
b) les actualités ☐
c) les documentaires ☐

6 Mon loisir préféré, c'est:
a) la télé ☐
b) la musique ☐
c) le cinéma ☐

7 J'aime écouter de la musique:
a) pop ☐
b) rock ☐
c) classique ☐

8 J'achète des CDs ou cassettes:
a) chaque semaine ☐
b) de temps en temps ☐
c) jamais (Je n'achète jamais ...) ☐

9 Mon chanteur préféré/Ma chanteuse préférée, c'est

_____

Q Say what your favourite pop group is.

3 Say your completed sentences out loud and try to memorise them.

A

WRITE

4 Now write five positive sentences about television programmes and music and five negative ones.

Exemple:

Je m'intéresse beaucoup aux documentaires sur les animaux.
Je ne m'intéresse pas du tout aux dessins animés.

Grammar – negatives

ne . . . pas:	Je **ne** regarde **pas** la télé. *(I don't wach TV.)*
ne . . . plus:	Je **ne** regarde **plus** les dessins animés. *(I don't watch cartoons anymore.)*
ne . . . jamais:	Je n´écoute **jamais** la radio. *(I never listen to the radio.)*
ne . . . rien:	Je **ne** sais **rien** au sujet de la musique. *(I don't know anything about music.)*
ne . . . personne:	Je **ne** connais **personne** qui aime le jazz. *(I don't know anybody who likes jazz.)*

B   At the cinema

SPEAK

1 Act out this dialogue at the cinema kiosk with a friend.

> Practise saying as much French as possible out loud to help improve your pronunciation.

– Bonsoir.
– Bonsoir. <u>Deux</u> places pour salle <u>trois</u>, s'il vous plaît.
– Oui, d'accord.
– Ça fait combien? Il y a des réductions pour les <u>étudiants</u>?
– Oui. Vous avez des pièces d'identité?
– Voilà.
– Merci. Alors, ça fait <u>dix-huit euros quarante.</u>
– Et le film commence à quelle heure?
– Il commence à <u>vingt heures dix.</u>
– Très bien. Et la séance finit à quelle heure?
– Elle finit à <u>vingt-deux heures trente.</u>
– Excusez-moi, mais c'est en version française?
– Non, désolé, c'est en version originale. Mais c'est sous-titré.
– Merci beaucoup.
– De rien.

How much re the tickets? ow long does he film last?

PRACTICE

Adapt the dialogue above to write a new dialogue with the following information:

- three tickets for cinema two
- reductions for children?
- tickets cost 24 euros
- film: 17:20–19:45
- in French

> Don't rush your answers in the oral exam – take your time to think through what you want to say. If you need some extra thinking time, use these French 'fillers': <u>Bien ...</u> <u>Alors ... Un moment ... Je réfléchis ...</u>

Work and lifestyle

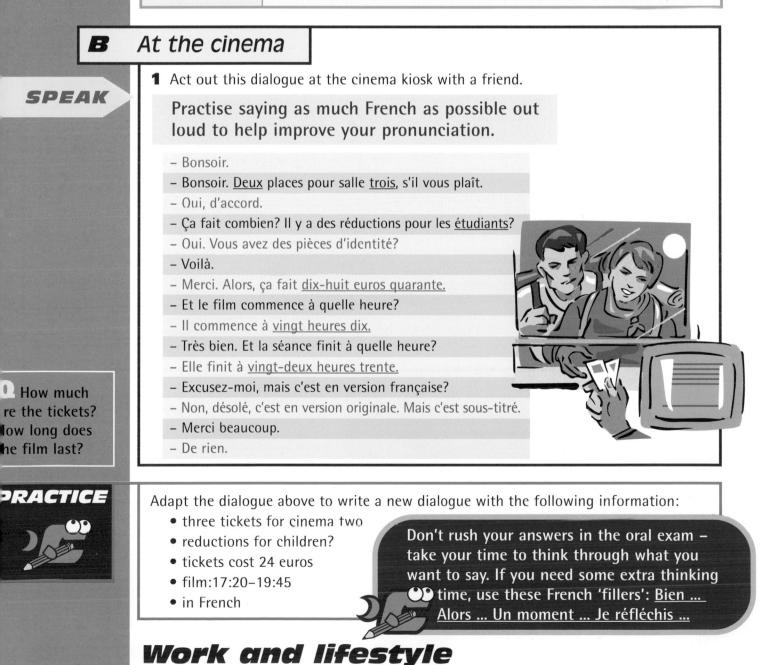

A Jobs

le boucher/la bouchère	butcher
le boulanger/la boulangère	baker
le caissier/la caissière	check-out assistant
le coiffeur/la coiffeuse	hairdresser
le directeur/la directrice	boss, head
un épicier/une épicière	grocer
le facteur/la factrice	postman/woman
le fermier/la fermière	farmer
un infirmier/une infirmière	nurse
le vendeur/la vendeuse	sales assistant
le serveur/la serveuse	waiter/waitress
un(e) employé(e) de banque	bank worker
un(e) employé(e) de bureau	office worker
le/la mécanicien(ne)	mechanic
un steward/une hôtesse de l'air	air steward/stewardess

Remember
Most jobs have two forms in French – one for a man and one for a woman: <u>le coiffeur</u> (male hairdresser), <u>la coiffeuse</u> (female hairdresser).

le chauffeur de taxi	taxi driver
le professeur	teacher
le gendarme	police officer
le dentiste	dentist
le médecin	doctor
un agent de police	police officer
un ingénieur	engineer
le propriétaire	landlord, owner
le pilote	pilot

Remember
This group of jobs are always <u>le</u>, whether the person is a man or a woman.

Mon père travaille comme (médecin).	My father works as a (doctor).
Ma tante est au chômage.	My aunt is unemployed.
Mon frère est sans travail.	My brother hasn't got a job.

B Places of work

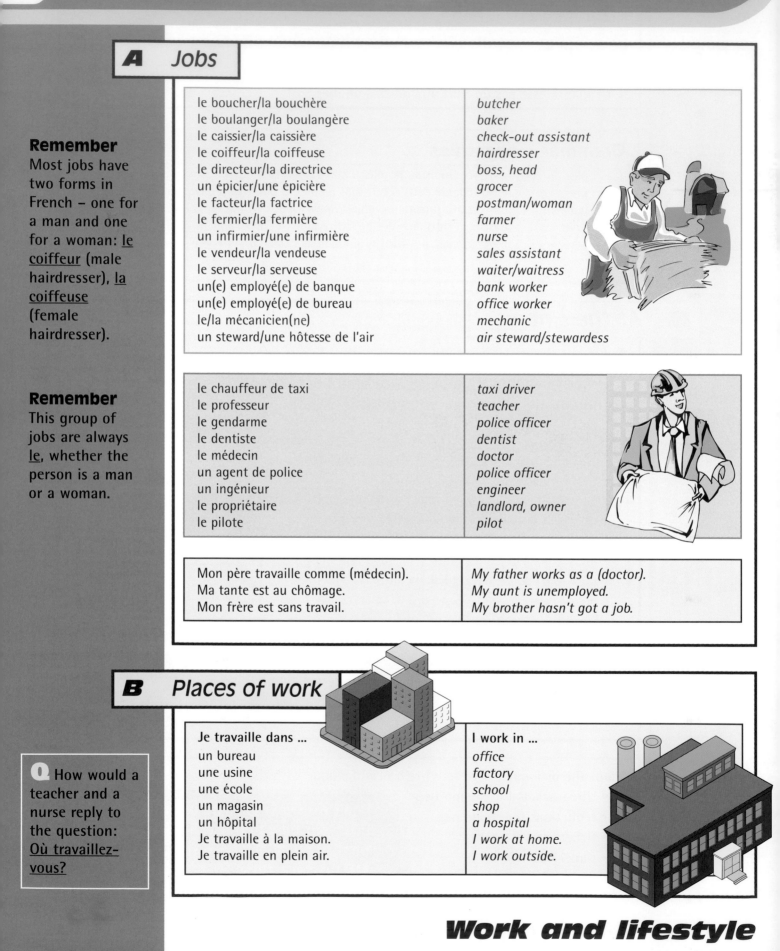

Je travaille dans ...	I work in ...
un bureau	office
une usine	factory
une école	school
un magasin	shop
un hôpital	a hospital
Je travaille à la maison.	I work at home.
Je travaille en plein air.	I work outside.

Q How would a teacher and a nurse reply to the question: <u>Où travaillez-vous?</u>

Work and lifestyle

Grammar – travailler – to work

je travaille	*I work*	nous travaillons	*we work*
tu travailles	*you (informal) work*	vous travaillez	*you (formal) work*
il/on travaille	*he/one works*	ils travaillent	*they (masculine) work*
elle travaille	*she works*	elles travaillent	*they (feminine) work*
j'ai travaillé	*I worked*	je travaillerai	*I will work*

PRACTICE

Unscramble the anagrams to find the jobs.

ⓐ oruspesefr

ⓓ lgounrebèa

ⓔ cimdeén

ⓑ rfremie

ⓕ euctfar

ⓒ lteopi

ⓖ *vuseeser*

Q For which jobs can you work out whether it is for a man or a woman?

Work and lifestyle

THE BARE BONES

➤ Filling in a CV, identity form or application form all require the same sorts of personal information.

➤ Make sure you know all the French words for the jobs your family does.

A Job descriptions

READ

1 With jobs you **don't need to add a word for 'a'** in French: *Je suis plombier* means 'I am a plumber'.

2 C'est quel métier? Ecrivez les phrases.
What job do they do? Write sentences.

Exemple: a On est professeur.

a On travaille dans une école. Il faut aimer les enfants pour faire ce métier.

b Pour ce métier il faut travailler souvent pendant la nuit. On travaille dans un hôpital et on soigne les malades.

c C'est un emploi pour les gens qui adorent les voitures! On travaille dans un garage.

d Cet emploi est très intéressant. On voyage tout le temps mais on passe beaucoup de temps dans les aéroports. Il faut être poli avec les gens dans l'avion.

Q Write your own definitions for these jobs: <u>coiffeur/ coiffeuse, dentiste, boulanger/ boulangère.</u>

Grammar – il faut + infinitive verb

il faut travailler	*you have to work*

B Family jobs

Remember
Another way of saying you have to do something is to use <u>devoir</u> (<u>tu dois travailler</u> you have to work).

1 Lisez le texte et trouvez les quatre phrases vraies. Read the text and find the four true sentences.

Ma mère est professeur et elle travaille dans mon école – c'est pénible pour moi, ça! Mon père est au chômage en ce moment, mais il cherche un emploi comme mécanicien. Mon oncle travaille dans un bureau – il est journaliste et il écrit des articles sur le sport. Ma tante ne travaille pas parce qu'elle est malade – je trouve ça dommage. Mon grand-père était gendarme à Toulouse, mais depuis deux ans il est en retraite. Son emploi était très dangereux.

a La mère de Martin va à la même école que Martin.

b Le père de Martin travaille comme mécanicien en ce moment.

c L'oncle de Martin s'intéresse au sport.

d L'oncle de Martin fait son travail dans un garage.

e La tante de Martin a une maladie.

f Le grand-père de Martin n'a jamais travaillé.

g Le grand-père de Martin ne travaille plus.

READ

Q What happened to Martin's grandfather two years ago?

☐ ☐ ☐ ☐

Work and lifestyle

C A CV

1 The personal details on this CV could also be useful if you had to **fill in an ID form, an application form** or **leave your details** at the lost property office.

2 Remplissez le formulaire avec les détails ci-dessous.
Fill in the CV with the details below.

READ

CURRICULUM VITAE

1 Nom: _Alain Dupont_
2 Age:
3 Date de naissance:
4 Lieu de naissance:
5 Nationalité:
6 Père (nom/emploi):
7 Mère (nom/emploi):
8 Adresse (code postal):
9 Numéro de téléphone:
10 Formation:
11 Loisirs:
12 Emploi à temps partiel:
13 Emploi idéal:

Details column:
- ordinateurs/le cinéma
- dix-huit ans
- français
- programmeur
- Alain Dupont
- Toulouse
- Herbert Dupont (journaliste)
- distribue les journaux
- Karine Dupont (vendeuse)
- 60.98.67.97
- 10, rue de Breil, 35051 Rennes
- 3 décembre 1989
- 1994–2001: l'école primaire à Toulouse;
- de 2001: Lycée St.-Germain, Rennes

Q Can you write out another CV with your own details?

Fill in the gaps you are sure of first and cross them out on the exam paper as you do so. Then look at what's left over and try to make sensible guesses as to what goes in the remaining spaces.

PRACTICE

Write a sentence about yourself for each of the thirteen headings on the CV above.

Exemple: 1 Je m'appelle Juliette Blanc.
2 J'ai seize ans –

Work and lifestyle

Teenage work - vocabulary

A Helping at home

Je fais la vaisselle.	I wash up.
Je fais les courses.	I do the shopping.
Je mets la table.	I lay the table.
Je débarrasse la table.	I clear the table.
Je fais le jardinage.	I do the gardening.
Je fais le repassage.	I do the ironing.
Je nettoie la maison/les fenêtres.	I clean the house/windows.
Je range ma chambre.	I tidy my room.
Je lave mes vêtements.	I wash my clothes.
Je sors la poubelle.	I take the rubbish out.
Je passe l'aspirateur.	I vacuum.
Je fais la cuisine.	I cook meals.
Je prépare les repas.	I cook the meals.
le petit déjeuner/déjeuner/dîner	breakfast/lunch/dinner
le week-end	at the weekend
toujours	always
tous les jours	every day
de temps en temps	sometimes
ne ... jamais	never
J'aime aider à la maison.	I like helping at home.
Je n'aime pas faire le ménage.	I don't like housework.
Je ne passe jamais l'aspirateur.	I never vacuum.

Q What do you like and dislike doing at home? Go through the list of tasks, saying sentences: J'aime/Je n'aime pas faire/mettre/ranger ...

Grammar – present tense singular

	I	you	he/she/one
aimer (*to like*)	j'aime	tu aimes	il/elle/on aime
ranger (*to tidy*)	je range	tu ranges	il/elle/on range
laver (*to wash*)	je lave	tu laves	il/elle/on lave
nettoyer (*to clean*)	je nettoie	tu nettoies	il/elle/on nettoie
faire (*to do*)	je fais	tu fais	il/elle/on fait
mettre (*to put*)	je mets	tu mets	il/elle/on met

Remember
Regular –er verbs ending in –oyer change the y to i before e.

B Work experience

J'ai fait un stage d'entreprise.	I did work experience.
J'ai aidé les clients.	I helped the clients.
J'ai travaillé dans une usine.	I worked in a factory.
J'ai organisé des rendez-vous.	I organised meetings.
J'ai livré/tapé des lettres.	I delivered/typed letters.
J'ai répondu au téléphone.	I answered the phone.
J'ai fait des photocopies.	I did photocopying.
J'ai travaillé sur l'ordinateur.	I worked on the computer.
J'ai travaillé dans une grande usine.	I worked in a big factory.

Remember
Copy five sentences, then check your spellings. When you're copying from the exam paper, take care with spellings.

Work and lifestyle

C Part-time work and pocket money

Je fais du babysitting.	*I babysit.*
Je distribue les journaux.	*I deliver newspapers.*
Je travaille dans un bureau.	*I work in an office.*
Je fais du jardinage.	*I do gardening.*
Je travaille comme garçon de café.	*I work as a waiter.*
Je commence à huit heures.	*I start at eight o'clock.*
Je finis à quatre heures.	*I finish at four o'clock.*
Je travaille six heures au magasin.	*I work six hours in a shop.*
Je travaille dans un supermarché.	*I work in a supermarket.*
Je travaille le samedi/le week-end.	*I work on Saturdays/at the weekend.*
Je gagne six euros de l'heure.	*I earn six euros an hour.*
Je fais des économies.	*I'm saving.*
Je n'ai pas de petit emploi.	*I haven't got a job.*
C'est varié/intéressant.	*It's varied/interesting.*
C'était fatigant/bien payé.	*It was tiring/well-paid.*
Mes parents me donnent huit euros par semaine.	*My parents give me eight euros a week.*
Je reçois trente euros par mois.	*I get thirty euros a month.*
Je ne reçois pas d'argent de poche.	*I don't get any pocket money.*

Remember

Learn set phrases but be prepared to adapt them in the exam. For example, **je fais du jardinage** can be changed to **il fait du jardinage** or **je ne fais pas de jardinage** very easily.

PRACTICE

What part-time work do these people do? Write sentences.

Exemple: Jean fait du babysitting.

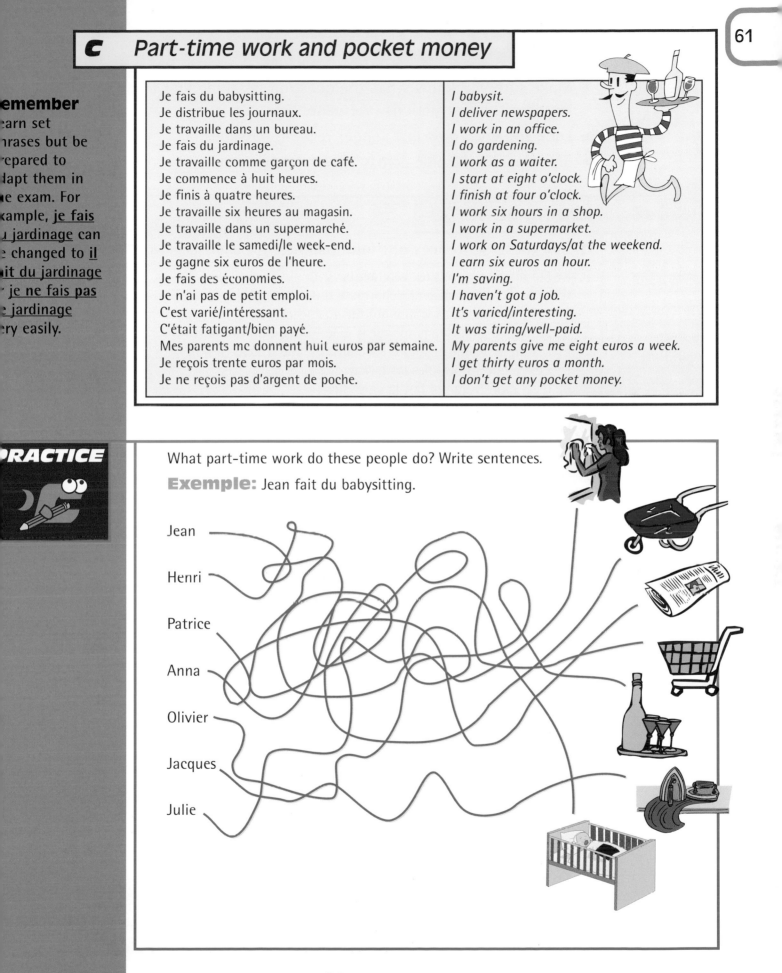

Jean

Henri

Patrice

Anna

Olivier

Jacques

Julie

Work and lifestyle

THE BARE BONES

➤ Make sure you know what the question is asking you to do by learning the instructions (see page 98).

➤ Look for key words in a longer reading passage.

➤ Be prepared to come across adverts in the exam.

A Helping at home

SPEAK

1 **Say these sentences out loud** and check you understand what they mean.

a Ma mère lave tous les vêtements.
b Le week-end, ma sœur débarrasse toujours la table.
c Dans la famille, c'est moi qui fais la cuisine.
d Je ne fais jamais le jardinage – je le trouve trop fatigant.
e Ma mère n'aime pas faire les courses – elle trouve ça nul.
f Est-ce que tu nettoies les fenêtres?
g C'est mon frère qui fait la vaisselle.
h Mon beau-frère ne range jamais sa chambre.
i J'aime sortir la poubelle.
j Mon père déteste passer l'aspirateur.

Q Who does the washing up in this household?

2 Now match those sentences with the pictures of chores below. Look quickly for the **verb** (the doing word) in each sentence – **that'll give you a clue**. Ignore the time expressions and opinions as you don't need them to complete the task.

> Work out what you are looking for in tasks like this and then locate that information.

READ

3 Faites correspondre les phrases a–j aux images 1–10.
Match the sentences a–j to the pictures 1–10.

Q Underline the key words in each sentence which helped you match it to the pictures.

Work and lifestyle

B Job adverts

READ

1 In the next activity, you'll be matching three adverts to three speech bubbles. **Don't worry if you don't understand every word. Look for similarities** between any of the **words in the speech bubbles** and the **words in the adverts.** For example, *nature* might be connected to *jardin*. What other connections can you find?

Q When does Virginie prefer to work?

> Scan the texts for key words and underline them.

Virginie: Ma passion, c'est la nature. J'adore travailler en plein air. Je me lève très tôt parce que je préfère travailler le matin.

Julie: Je suis l'aînée et il me faut garder mes petits frères. Ils ont trois et cinq ans. Le week-end je fais du babysitting pour les voisins. J'adore ça!

Matthieu: Moi, j'aide beaucoup à la maison: je fais la cuisine, je nettoie ma chambre et de temps en temps je tonds la pelouse. Ça me plaît.

```
1 ON RECHERCHE UNE PERSONNE
  CAPABLE
  (n'importe quel âge) pour
  nous aider dans notre jardin
  d'herbes aromatiques – sept
  heures par jour(06h00–13h00)
  Tél: 03 52 87 94.

2 NOTRE HÔTEL RECHERCHE:
  PERSONNEL ...
  ·   entre 16–25 ans
  ·   pour travailler dans notre
      hôtel renommé
  ·   juillet–octobre
  ·   emploi varié!
  ☎ 65 78 95 45

3 ON RECHERCHE: JEUNE PERSONNE
  (âge: minimum dix-huit ans)
  pour nos deux filles
  adorables (deux et six ans)

  09h00–5h00 (juillet et août)

  Contactez-nous au: 34 65 87 12
```

Q Which positions could a 17-year-old apply for?

2 Faites correspondre les jeunes gens aux petites annonces.
Match the young people to the adverts.

Virginie ☐   Julie ☐   Matthieu ☐

PRACTICE

Now have a go at answering these questions on the above text in English.

a   Does Virginie get up early?
b   Has Julie got an older sister?
c   Does Matthieu mow the lawn?
d   What children need looking after?
e   When is the hotel work available?
f   What hours' work are available at the herb nursery?

You can scribble notes on the exam paper or underline and cross things out – it's not like a textbook in class.

Work and lifestyle

Health – vocabulary

A Illness

Remember

When you're revising vocabulary, draw pictures or symbols to help you remember the words.

Remember

If you injure a part of your body, 'my' is normally translated by le, la or les: Je me suis cassé la jambe means 'I've broken my leg'.

Je me sens malade./Je suis malade.	I feel ill.
J'ai mal au cœur.	I feel sick.
J'ai mal à la gorge.	I've got a sore throat.
J'ai mal à la tête.	I've got a headache.
J'ai mal au ventre.	I've got stomach ache.
J'ai mal aux dents.	I've got toothache.
Le bras/pied me fait mal.	My arm/foot hurts.
Les jambes me font mal.	My legs hurt.
Je me suis coupé(e) le doigt.	I've cut my finger.
Je me suis cassé(e) la jambe.	I've broken my leg.
Je suis enrhumé(e).	I've got a cold.
J'ai un rhume.	I've got a cold
J'ai la grippe.	I've got the flu.
J'ai de la fièvre.	I've got a temperature.
J'ai envie de vomir.	I want to be sick.
Je suis fatigué(e).	I'm tired.
Va chez le docteur/à l'hôpital.	Go to the doctor/hospital.
Va chez le pharmacien.	Go to the chemist.
Prends quatre comprimés chaque jour.	Take four tablets a day.
Prenez ce médicament.	Take this medicine.
Prends du sirop/des pastilles pour la gorge.	Take some syrup/throat pastilles.
C'est grave?	Is it serious?

B Parts of the body

Q Sketch a person and label it with the correct French words for all the parts of the body.

le corps	body	la jambe	leg
la tête	head	le genou	knee
le cou	neck	le pied	foot
une oreille	ear	un estomac	stomach
le nez	nose	le bras	arm
la bouche	mouth	la main	hand
un œil (les yeux)	eyes (eyes)	le doigt	finger
le dos	back		

Work and lifestyle

C Fruit and vegetables

les fruits	*fruit*	un abricot	*apricot*
un ananas	*pineapple*	un citron	*lemon*
une banane	*banana*	une cerise	*cherry*
une fraise	*strawberry*	une framboise	*raspberry*
une orange	*orange*	une pêche	*peach*
une pomme	*apple*	une poire	*pear*
du raisin	*grapes*	une tomate	*tomato*
les légumes	*vegetables*	un chou-fleur	*cauliflower*
une carotte	*carrot*	des pommes de terre	*potatoes*
une salade	*salad, lettuce*	des champignons	*mushrooms*
des haricots verts	*green beans*	des petits pois	*peas*

D Higher numbers

soixante et un	61	soixante-deux	62	soixante-trois	63
soixante-quatre	64	soixante-cinq	65	soixante-six	66
soixante-sept	67	soixante-huit	68	soixante-neuf	69
soixante-dix	70	soixante et onze	71	soixante-douze	72
soixante-treize	73	soixante-quatorze	74	soixante-quinze	75
soixante-seize	76	soixante-dix-sept	77	soixante-dix-huit	78
soixante-dix-neuf	79	quatre-vingts	80	quatre-vingt-un	81
quatre-vingt-deux	82	quatre-vingt-trois	83	quatre-vingt-quatre	84
quatre-vingt-dix	90	quatre-vingt-onze	91	quatre-vingt-douze	92
quatre-vingt-treize	93	quatre-vingt-quatorze	94	quatre-vingt-quinze	95
quatre-vingt-seize	96	quatre-vingt-dix-sept	97	quatre-vingt-dix-huit	98
cent	100	cent un	101	deux cents	200
mille	1000	deux mille	2000	deux mille dix	2010

How do you say these numbers in French: 68, 99, 112, 2456?

E Quantities

une boîte de (tomates)	*a box of/a tin of (tomatoes)*
une douzaine de (pommes)	*a dozen (apples)*
cinq cents grammes de (pommes)	*500 grammes of (apples)*
un kilo de (pommes de terre)	*a kilo of (potatoes)*
un peu de sel	*a bit of/a little salt*
beaucoup/plein de (tomates)	*lots of (tomatoes)*
quelques/des (poires)	*some (pears)*
plusieurs (cerises)	*several (cherries)*

PRACTICE See if you can count to one hundred without stopping in French.

Work and lifestyle

Health

THE BARE BONES
➤ Always read all the answers through in multiple choice questions.

➤ Make sure you know how to ask for quantities of fruit and vegetables – not just the item itself.

➤ Check you know how to say numbers above 60.

A   Illnesses

READ

1 With multiple choice questions, **always read all the possible answers carefully** – don't get distracted by thinking you know the answer straight away.

2   Choisissez la bonne réponse. Choose the correct answer.

1 Si on est malade on va:
- a) à l'école ☐
- b) à la bibliothèque ☐
- c) chez le médecin. ☐

2 Quand on a mal aux dents on va:
- a) chez le dentiste ☐
- b) chez le docteur ☐
- c) chez le pharmacien. ☐

3 Un docteur travaille:
- a) dans une usine ☐
- b) à l'hôpital ☐
- c) dans un bureau. ☐

4 Quand on a mal aux mains on a des difficultés à:
- a) marcher ☐
- b) manger ☐
- c) écrire. ☐

5 Si on a mal au pied on a des problèmes à:
- a) parler ☐
- b) courir ☐
- c) boire. ☐

6 Si on a la grippe on:
- a) reste au lit ☐
- b) va à la disco ☐
- c) va au cinéma. ☐

7 Si on est enrhumé, on achète:
- a) du poulet ☐
- b) du vin ☐
- c) des mouchoirs. ☐

Remember
If you really don't know the answer to a multiple choice question, have a guess – that way you'll at least have a chance of getting it right.

Q Say that you've got a cold and a temperature and your back hurts in French.

Grammar – faire mal

singular word	=	le pied me **fait** mal
plural word	=	les pieds me **font** mal

Work and lifestyle

B Buying fruit and vegetables

SPEAK

1 You need to know **quantities** of things to go shopping (see page 65 for numbers) for fruit and vegetables. Look at this list and see if you can ask for the items on it in French.

Always say <u>s'il vous plaît</u> (please) and <u>merci</u> (thank you) when you're doing a shopping role play.

Remember
Whenever you come across a number – on a car or sign, or in a book – try to say it out loud in French.

Shopping list

300 grammes of green beans

half a kilo of carrots

a kilo of potatoes

a dozen pears

a box of tomatoes

some raspberries

two cauliflowers

00 grammes de

un demi kilo de

deux kilos de

une boîte de

une douzaine de

des

PRACTICE

Find the opposite pairs of sentences.

Exemple: a 5

a Je suis en superforme.

b Je ne sais pas combien je pèse.

c C'est mauvais pour la santé.

d Je dois suivre un régime.

e J'ai perdu deux kilos cette semaine.

f Je veux grossir.

g Je fais du sport tous les jours.

h Je ne fume pas.

i Je suis végétarien(ne).

1 J'ai pris dix kilos pendant les vacances.

2 Je fume trois cigarettes chaque jour.

3 Je déteste faire du sport – c'est fatigant.

4 J'aime bien manger du poulet.

5 Je ne suis pas en bonne santé.

6 Je mange n'importe quoi.

7 Je me pèse tous les jours.

8 C'est bon pour la santé.

9 Je veux maigrir.

Don't spend all your time on the first question in the exam and not have time to finish the paper.

Work and lifestyle

A Food

Remember
Write two lists of these food items on the right: one for food you like and one for food you dislike.

la viande	meat	le bœuf	beef
le jambon	ham	le poulet	chicken
le porc	pork	le veau	veal
la saucisse	sausage	le saucisson	cold sausage
le pâté	paté	le fromage	cheese
le poisson	fish	les fruits de mer	seafood
un œuf/les œufs	egg/eggs	le pain	bread
les pâtes	pasta	le riz	rice
le yaourt	yoghurt	la glace	ice cream

J'aime (le steak).	I like (steak).
Je n'aime pas (le bifteck).	I don't like (beef steak).
J'adore (la glace).	I love (ice cream).
Je déteste (les chips).	I hate (crisps).
Je ne mange jamais de (fromage).	I never eat (cheese).
un paquet de (chips)	a packet of (crisps)
un pot de (confiture)	a jar of (jam)
une tranche de (jambon)	a slice of (ham)
un morceau de (gâteau)	a piece of (cake)

B Drinks

la bière	beer	le cidre	cider
le vin rouge	red wine	le vin blanc	white wine
le coca	cola	la limonade	lemonade
une eau minérale	mineral water	un Orangina	orangina
un café	coffee	avec lait/sucre	with milk/sugar
un chocolat chaud	hot chocolate	un thé	tea

Q How would you ask for a cup of tea with sugar and milk?

une tasse de (chocolat)	a cup of (chocolate)
un litre de lait	a litre of milk
une bouteille de (limonade)	a bottle of (lemonade)

C At a restaurant

Avez-vous une table pour deux personnes?	Have you got a table for two people?
Je voudrais réserver une table pour dix personnes.	I'd like to book a table for ten people.
Pour quand?	For when?
Pour samedi soir, à huit heures.	For Saturday night at 8pm.
Désolé, c'est complet.	I'm sorry, we're full.

Work and lifestyle

C

Monsieur!/Mademoiselle!	Waiter!/Waitress!
Avez-vous la carte?	Have you got a menu?
Qu'est-ce que vous prenez?	What would you like?
C'est quoi, la spécialité?	What is the special?
C'est du poulet avec une sauce aux tomates.	It's chicken with a tomato sauce.
Un croque-monsieur, s'il vous plaît.	A toasted sandwich, please.
Pour commencer, je prendrai les fruits de mer.	For starters, I'll have the seafood.
Qu'est-ce que vous désirez comme boisson?	What would you like to drink?
Je voudrais du vin rouge/blanc.	I'd like some red/white wine.
Je vais prendre un coca.	I'll have a cola.
Bon appétit!	Enjoy your meal!
L'addition, s'il vous plaît.	The bill, please.
Le service (n')est (pas) compris.	Service is (not) included.

Remember
Revise how to ask the questions as well as the items of vocabulary – you may need to ask questions if you get a restaurant role play.

D Restaurant complaints

Je n'ai pas de couteau.	I haven't got a knife.
Cette cuillère/fourchette est sale.	This spoon/fork is dirty.
Cette tasse est très vieille.	This cup is very old.
Il y a de la confiture sur l'assiette.	There's jam on the plate.
La soupe est froide.	The soup is cold.
Le poisson sent mauvais.	The fish smells bad.
Ce poulet a un goût désagréable.	This chicken has an unpleasant taste.
Cette crêpe est trop sucrée.	This crepe is too sweet.
Il y a trop de poivre/sel.	There's too much pepper/salt.
Où est la moutarde?	Where's the mustard?
Il n'y a pas de vinaigre.	There's no vinegar.
J'ai commandé un vin rouge mais on m'a donné ce vin blanc.	I ordered red wine but I was given this white wine.
J'ai commandé le plat principal mais j'ai reçu des pâtes.	I ordered the main dish but got pasta.
J'ai dû attendre une heure pour ma pizza.	I had to wait an hour for my pizza.
Il y a une erreur dans l'addition.	There's a mistake in the bill.

Make three complaints about a meal at a restaurant.

PRACTICE

What's in these dishes? Choose the right answer each time.

1 une omelette: a) des pâtes ☐ b) des œufs ☐ c) de la bière ✔
2 les chips: a) du riz ☐ b) du poisson ☐ c) des pommes de terre ☐
3 le saucisson: a) du porc ☐ b) du fromage ☐ c) des pois ☐
4 un potage de légumes: a) des carottes ☐ b) du bœuf ☐ c) du chocolat ☐
5 un gâteau: a) des moules ☐ b) du cidre ☐ c) de la farine et du beurre ☐
6 une tartine: a) du pain ☐ b) des pâtes ☐ c) du coca ☐
7 la limonade: a) des pommes ☐ b) des oranges ☐ c) des citrons ☐

Work and lifestyle

Food and drink

THE BARE BONES

➤ If you know lots of vocabulary items for food and drink, use them in the exam by giving more than one detail in your work.

➤ Don't translate reading passages in the exam word for word – you won't have time and it just isn't necessary.

A   Food and drink items

WRITE

1   Cherchez douze choses à manger ou à boire. Find twelve words for food and drink items in the grid.

Remember
Learn the twelve words and test yourself on them in a week's time.

T	A	B	R	F	P	O	M	M	E	C
H	T	I	P	O	U	L	E	T	H	R
É	I	S	S	A	Q	E	W	S	J	O
V	X	C	Z	O	E	U	F	O	H	I
F	H	U	P	A	I	N	K	U	L	S
P	O	I	S	S	O	N	T	P	C	S
V	W	T	M	K	G	R	U	E	A	A
D	C	H	O	C	O	L	A	T	F	N
J	A	M	B	O	N	T	Y	P	É	T

B   What I eat

SPEAK

1 Look at these sentence beginnings and see if you can finish them off.

Try and give two or three items in your answers rather than the minimum of one.

Exemple: a Pour le petit déjeuner je mange des céréales avec du lait et du pain avec de la confiture et du beurre. Le week-end je mange souvent un œuf et du jambon. Je bois toujours du thé avec du sucre et du lait.

Q Write down four food items you like and four you dislike:
J'aime manger du/de la/de l'/ des ...
Je n'aime pas manger ...

a Pour le petit déjeuner je mange ... et je bois ...

b Pour le déjeuner je mange ... et je bois ...

c Pour le dîner je mange ... et je bois ...

Work and lifestyle

Grammar – du, de la, de l', des

Use **du, de la, des, de l'** instead of **le/la/les** when talking about things you eat/drink.

du	masculine words	→ du poulet, du jambon
de la	feminine words	→ de la limonade, de la bière
des	plural words	→ des croissants, des tartines
de l'	words starting with a, e, i, o, u, h	→ de l'eau minérale, de l'œuf

Remember
du, de l', de la and des are used with food: je bois du café means I'm drinking (some) coffee.

C Cafés

READ

1 Don't translate every word in a reading activity – that will take too long. Scan through all the texts to see what the activity is about first.

Always look for the key words as you scan a text.

JEAN ☐

J'adore le fast-food, et je mange de la viande chaque jour.

TIM ☐

J'aime bien les gâteaux et je voudrais boire du thé.

KATHERINE ☐

C'est le matin et je suis fatiguée – j'ai grand faim aussi!

Café des Artistes
- Café au choix
- Thé au lait ou citron
- Chocolat chaud avec crème
- Eau minérale
- Gâteau maison
- Pâtisseries
- Glaces

Notre spécialité du jour:
Mille-feuilles

Restaurant Au Coin

Aujourd'hui:
petit déjeuner

œuf à la coque

2 croissants

jus d'orange

café

(2)

Chez Monsieur H.

Hamburger-Fromage
Saucisse maison
Poulet avec pommes frites et haricots verts
Coca et limonade

(3)

Q Jean likes fast food and meat – which food items would he like from these menus?

Q Why does the word **matin** from Katherine's speech bubble go with **petit déjeuner** from the menu?

2 Faites correspondre les bulles aux cartes. Match the speech bubbles to the menus.

Match the speech bubbles and menus you're sure of first – you don't have to find Jean's first just because it's the first in the activity.

PRACTICE

Write about what these people eat for lunch.

Exemple: Paul mange du poulet et de la glace.

Frank – sausage and rice and yoghurt

Yves – pasta and soup and chocolate

Paul – chicken and ice cream

Emilie – cheese and bread and lemonade

Work and lifestyle

A The environment

Remember
Use the phrase
<u>à mon avis</u>
(in my opinion)
when writing
about other
topics too.

Il y a trop de circulation.	*There's too much traffic.*
Il y a trop de camions sur les routes.	*There are too many lorries on the roads.*
Les embouteillages sont partout/terribles.	*The traffic jams are everywhere/terrible.*
L'heure d'affluence est un grand problème.	*The rush hour is a big problem.*
La qualité de l'air est atroce.	*The air quality is terrible.*
La ville est très polluée.	*The city is very polluted.*
Il y a des déchets partout.	*There's rubbish everywhere.*
Les trottoirs sont sales.	*The pavements are dirty.*
A mon avis on utilise trop d'énergie.	*In my opinion we use too much energy.*
Les animaux sont en danger.	*Animals are in danger.*
Les plantes ont besoin de protection.	*Plants need protection.*
La pollution est un problème mondial.	*Pollution is a worldwide problem.*
Je porte des bouteilles au centre de recyclage.	*I take bottles to the recycling centre.*
Je prends les transports en commun.	*I use public transport.*
Je vais partout à vélo.	*I go everywhere by bike.*
Je me douche tous les matins.	*I shower every morning.*
Je réduis la température du chauffage central	*I turn down the central heating.*
Je ferme les portes/fenêtres.	*I close doors/windows.*
Je protège les plantes/animaux en danger.	*I protect endangered plants/animals.*
La pollution de la mer m'inquiète.	*Sea pollution worries me.*
L'environnement m'ennuie.	*The environment bores me.*

B Smoking

Remember
Cover the English
column and say
the English as
you look at the
French column.
Check that you
got them right.

Je fume.	*I smoke.*
Je ne fume pas.	*I don't smoke.*
Je fume dix cigarettes par jour.	*I smoke ten cigarettes a day.*
Je n'ai pas peur du cancer.	*I'm not afraid of cancer.*
Je me suis habitué(e) à fumer.	*I've got used to smoking.*
Je suis pour/contre le tabac.	*I'm for/against smoking.*

C Alcohol

Je ne bois pas d'alcool.	I don't drink alcohol.
Je bois du vin/du cidre.	I drink wine/cider.
Je bois de la bière chaque jour.	I drink beer every day.
J'ai envie d'arrêter de boire.	I want to give up drinking.
L'alcoolisme, c'est un grand problème.	Alcoholism is a big problem.
Il y a beaucoup de cosummation d'alcool par les mineurs.	There is a lot of under-age drinking
Je suis devenu(e) alcoolique.	I've become addicted to alcohol.
Tous mes amis boivent de l'alcool.	All my friends drink alcohol.
L'alcool ne m'intéresse pas.	Alcohol doesn't interest me.

Remember
Copy out words and phrases that you have difficulty with but remember to always check the spellings.

D Drugs

Je ne prends pas de drogue	I don't take any drugs.
J'ai peur de devenir drogué(e).	I'm afraid of becoming a drug addict.
Je dois perdre l'habitude.	I've got to kick the habit.
C'est une maladie.	It's a sickness.
Je fais ça tous les jours/le week-end/pas souvent.	I do that every day/at the weekend/rarely.
Tous mes ami(e)s font ça le week-end.	All my friends do it at the weekend.
Mes ami(e)s m'encouragent.	My friends encourage me.
Je trouve ça dangereux.	I find it dangerous.

Remember
The more vocabulary you revise before the exam, the easier it will be, so try to revise at least ten words or phrases a day.

PRACTICE

Read these sentences and tick the correct box to show what they are about.

	tabac	alcool	drogues
a J'étais adolescent(e) quand j'ai allumé ma première cigarette.			
b Chez nous on boit tous les soirs.			
c Moi, je suis devenu drogué(e) il y a cinq ans.			
d J'aime aller aux boums pour danser, rencontrer des jeunes et boire beaucoup.			
e J'aime boire de l'alcool parce que c'est une façon de faire 'comme les grands'.			
f J'affirme ma liberté quand je fume de la marihuana.			
g Je veux arrêter de fumer parce que c'est mauvais pour la santé.			
h Il faut dire non à la drogue.			

Which three activities are mentioned in sentence d?

Young person in society

THE BARE BONES

➤ Learn some stock phrases to use in a variety of topics.

➤ Be prepared to cope with some unfamiliar vocabulary in the Higher exam.

➤ Knowing how to express your opinion is an important aspect of the exam, and can be used in most topics.

A Learning some stock phrases – environment

SPEAK

Remember
Try to learn and use <u>C'est un grand problème</u> (it's a big problem), <u>Je trouve ça effrayant</u> (I find that frightening), <u>C'est insupportable</u> (it's intolerable).

1 Before you go into the speaking exam, it is important that you try to **learn a few phrases from each of the topics** you cover in class.

> Don't go for an overload when you're learning phrases as you're better off knowing three phrases accurately than ten phrases inaccurately or only partly.

2 Look at these phrases for the environment and check you understand them. Then learn them off by heart.

La terre se réchauffe – et ça **c'est un grand problème.**

Nous polluons notre planète et **je trouve ça effrayant.**

Des animaux sont menacés. **C'est insupportable.**

Je m'inquiète parce qu'il y a un trou dans la couche d'ozone.

B Phrases for discussing issues

READ

Remember
You can use these phrases in the writing exam as well as the speaking exam.

1 Faites correspondre les phrases. Match the sentences.

1 Je crois/pense/trouve que (l'environnement est un sujet important). `f`

2 Je suis contre (la drogue). ☐

3 Je suis pour (le recyclage). ☐

4 Il faut examiner les avantages et les inconvénients. ☐

5 Pour commencer il serait utile de (lister les faits). ☐

6 La situation s'aggrave chaque jour. ☐

7 A mon avis c'est un problème difficile à résoudre. ☐

8 Il faut discuter de ce problème grave. ☐

a I'm against (drugs).
b One has to look at the advantages and disadvantages.
c The situation gets worse every day.
d To start with it would be useful to (list the facts).
e In my opinion it's a difficult problem to solve.
f I believe/think/find that (the environment is an important topic).
g I'm for (recycling).
h One has to discuss this serious issue.

Young person in society

c An environmental action ⓗ

READ

1 In the Higher paper there will be some unfamiliar vocabulary that you'll have to cope with but **don't panic as you can probably work some of it out once you start reading.** Read this letter through and underline anything you don't understand. Then use the tips below to see if you can work out any meanings.

ⓗ

> Québec,
>
> le 5 juin
>
> Chère Sharon,
>
> Merci de ta lettre. C'est toujours avec plaisir que je te lis. En ce moment je suis très occupée car je viens de m'inscrire à mon école à un groupe qui travaille sur l'environnement. Nous faisons un projet sur le recyclage. Aussi avons-nous plein de poubelles spéciales recyclage. Maintenant tous les élèves trient leurs détritus. Il y a des poubelles pour les piles électriques, le papier, le carton, les canettes en aluminium et il y a en a même pour les déchets organiques (ces derniers proviennent de la cantine). Notre groupe est responsable des poubelles et quand elles sont pleines, nous les emportons dans la cour de l'école! Tous les jours un camion passe les ramasser. La plupart des élèves sont très sérieux et jettent leurs déchets dans les poubelles spéciales. Le mardi c'est mon tour d'aider à nettoyer la cour de l'école. Et à ton école y a-t-il un système semblable?
>
> Ecris-moi vite pour me raconter. A bientôt.
>
> Amicalement,   Anna

Remember

The emphatic pronouns can be used in different ways. <u>C'est pour toi</u> (It's for you), <u>C'est moi</u> (It's me), <u>Ecris-lui</u> (Write to him).

Grammar – emphatic pronouns

moi	me	toi	you	lui	him, her	elle	her, she
nous	us, we	vous	you	eux	them, they (m. plural)	elles	them, they (f. plural)

2   Lisez la lettre et répondez aux questions en français.

Exemple: a Elle s'inscrit à un groupe qui travaille sur l'environnement.

ⓗ
a Pourquoi Anna est-elle très occupée en ce moment?
b Le projet s'intéresse à quoi?
c D'où viennent les déchets organiques?
d Qu'est-ce que le groupe d'Anna fait avec les poubelles?
e Quand est-ce que le camion ramasse les poubelles?
f Qu'est-ce qu'Anna fait le mardi?

> **Tips on words:** does it look like an English word? Is there a picture? Can you guess its meaning from the context? Can you answer without knowing it?

Q Write a reply to Anna's letter.

PRACTICE

Read these newspaper headlines. Which topic are they about?

a environment   [3]   b drug-taking   [ ]   c teenage drinking   [ ]
d smoking   [ ]   e homelessness   [ ]   f family problems   [ ]

1 **Il est interdit de fumer dans ce restaurant**
2 **1 ado sur 2 n'aime pas habiter chez ses parents**
3 **Sauvez votre planète!**   4 **Trop jeune pour boire de la bière**
5 **Les jeunes qui habitent sur nos rues**   6 **La lutte contre la drogue**

Young person in society

A Future plans

Cette année je vais passer des examens.	I'm taking exams this year.
L'année prochaine je passe en première.	I'm going into the sixth form next year.
Je vais passer le bac.	I'm going to do the bac (A-levels).
Je vais quitter l'école.	I'm going to leave school.
Je vais faire un apprentissage.	I'm going to do an apprenticeship.
J'espère faire des études à l'étranger.	I hope to study abroad.
Je chercherai un emploi sans responsabilité.	I'll look for a job with no responsibility.
Je chercherai un travail bien payé.	I'll look for a well-paid job.
Le salaire est important.	The salary is important.
Si j'ai de bonnes notes, j'irai à l'université/en fac.	If I get good grades, I'll go to university.
Si mes résultats sont mauvais, je redoublerai.	If my results are bad, I'll repeat the year.
J'aimerais bien travailler dans le commerce.	I'd like to work in business.
Mon ambition, c'est de travailler dans le tourisme.	My ambition is to work in tourism.
J'aimerais trouver un travail en plein air.	I'd like to find an outside job.
Je voudrais travailler à l'étranger.	I'd like to work abroad.
J'aimerais travailler en France.	I'd like to work in France.
Je voudrais me marier.	I'd like to get married.
Je voudrais bien avoir des enfants.	I'd like to have children.
Je ne sais pas quoi faire dans la vie.	I don't know what to do with my life.

Remember
When you talk about jobs in French, you don't normally use the French word for 'a': <u>Je voudrais être professeur</u> means 'I'd like to be a teacher'.

Grammar – verbs plus an infinitive

je voudrais/j'aimerais + infinitive	I would like to do something
je vais + infinitive	I will do something/I am going to do something (future)

B Adolescence

La vie de l'adolescent a beaucoup de soucis.	Adolescent life has many worries.
J'ai de gros problèmes à l'école/la maison.	I have big problems at school/home.
J'ai le droit de sortir le samedi soir.	I'm allowed to go out on Saturday nights.
Je n'ai jamais la permission d'aller aux fêtes.	I'm never allowed to go to parties.
On me brutalise.	I am bullied.
Les examens m'inquiètent.	I am worried/I worry about exams.
Je n'aime pas mon corps.	I don't like my body.
Je n'ai pas de petit(e) ami(e).	I haven't got a boyfriend/girlfriend.
Je n'ai pas de copains.	I don't have any friends.
Je n'ai pas d'argent.	I don't have any money.
Je veux quitter l'école.	I want to leave school.
J'ai peur du crime/de la violence.	I am afraid of crime/violence.
Je me sens tout(e) seul(e).	I feel alone.
Je ne peux pas communiquer avec les autres.	I can't communicate with others.
Je m'entends bien avec ma mère.	I get on well with my mum.
Je me dispute beaucoup avec mon père.	I argue a lot with my dad.
Ma mère n'aime pas mes piercings.	My mother doesn't like my piercings.

Q Make a list of the four biggest problems you face as a teenager.

Young person in society

B

Mes parents sont trop sévères.	*My parents are too strict.*
Mes parents me critiquent.	*My parents criticise me.*
Il y a peu/beaucoup de disputes chez nous.	*There are not many/lots of rows at home.*
La vie chez nous est difficile.	*Life at home is difficult.*

C **Problems at school**

Au collège on a trop de règles.	*There are too many rules at school.*
On ne doit pas porter de bijoux.	*You're not allowed to wear jewellery.*
On ne doit pas se maquiller.	*You're not allowed to wear make up.*
Il est interdit de fumer.	*You're not allowed to smoke.*
Il y a une bonne/mauvaise discipline.	*The discipline is good/bad.*
Les profs sont trop sévères.	*The teachers are too strict.*
Je suis toujours en retenue.	*I always get detention.*
Hier j'avais deux heures de retenue.	*I had two hours' detention yesterday.*
J'ai peur de la violence dans la salle de classe.	*I'm scared of violence in the classroom.*
L'enseignement souffre à cause de la violence.	*Lessons suffer due to the violence.*
Quelques élèves créent beaucoup de problèmes.	*A few pupils cause a lot of problems.*

Write down three things you are not allowed to do at school:
On ne doit pas ...

Grammar – future and conditional tenses

	will work	would work
je	travaille**rai**	travaille**rais**
tu	travaille**ras**	travaille**rais**
il/elle/on	travaille**ra**	travaille**rait**
nous	travaille**rons**	travaille**rions**
vous	travaille**rez**	travaille**riez**
ils/elles	travaille**ront**	travaille**raient**

j'**aurai** (*I will have*)	je **serai** (*I will be*),	j'**irai** (*I will go*)
je **ferai** (*I will do*)	je **verrai** (*I will see*)	je **pourrai** (*I will be able to*)
je **devrai** (*I will have to*)	je **voudrai** (*I will want to*)	je **viendrai** (*I will come*)

PRACTICE

Do you agree with these sentences about friendships? Write your own sentences a–g on the topic of friendships, using the expressions in red.

a **A mon avis** les copains sont très importants.

b **Je crois que** l'amitié est plus importante que la famille.

c **Je pense que** chacun a besoin d'amis.

d **A mon opinion** une meilleure amie doit être gentille et sportive.

e **Moi, je trouve qu'**un meilleur ami doit être bavard et amusant.

f **C'est important que** je ne me dispute pas avec mon meilleur ami.

g **Tout compte fait**, mes amis ne sont pas aussi importants que ma famille.

Young person in society

Adolescent life

THE BARE BONES

➤ Use any texts you revise from to pick out key phrases you can use later on to talk about your own situation.

➤ Make your answers as detailed as possible.

➤ You can give negative as well as positive opinions on a topic.

A **Adolescent life**

READ

1 Read what these teenagers think about life. Which one matches most closely your own situation? **Underline any phrases you might be able to use or adapt slightly in the exam** if you were talking/writing about yourself.

Jean-Philippe: Moi, j'ai seize ans et j'habite avec mon père et ma belle-mère. Mes parents m'énervent tout le temps parce qu'ils sont trop sévères – je n'ai jamais le droit de sortir le soir et je dois faire le ménage le week-end. A mon avis les jeunes doivent faire tout ce qu'ils veulent et la vie d'adolescent doit être joyeuse et sans soucis ni règles.

Isabelle: J'ai quinze ans et j'habite avec ma mère, mon beau-père et ses deux enfants. Je ne peux pas communiquer avec mon beau-père, mais je m'entends très bien avec ma mère et j'ai le droit de faire presque tout ce que je veux. Je sors toujours le week-end et je vais au cinéma ou chez mes amies trois fois par semaine. A mon avis, c'est important d'avoir beaucoup de liberté quand on est jeune.

Yasmine: Je suis fille unique et j'ai seize ans. Je trouve mes parents trop sévères – ils pensent que je suis encore leur petite fille et ils n'ont pas confiance en moi. Mes copains se moquent de moi parce que je dois rentrer à la maison après les cours et je n'ai jamais la permission de sortir le week-end ou le soir.

Vincent: J'ai dix-sept ans et depuis six mois j'habite avec ma petite amie et sa famille. Je m'entends très bien avec sa mère qui est très sympa – elle est assez jeune et elle comprend bien la vie d'ado. Par contre, mes parents étaient insupportables et on se disputait beaucoup – je ne pouvais plus habiter chez eux.

Q Make a list of all the family members mentioned in this article.

2 Go through the article again, and underline all **negative opinions in blue** and **positive opinions in red**.

3 Répondez aux questions. Answer the questions.

Look at the questions or activities that follow a reading text – they will often give you further clues as to meaning.

a Qui ne s'entend pas bien avec ses parents? .... *Jean-Philippe, Vincent, Yasmine*...........

b Qui doit rentrer à la maison après le collège? ....

c Qui n'habite plus avec ses parents? ....

d Qui est l'adolescent le plus âgé? ....

e Qui est l'adolescent le plus jeune? ....

f Qui a beaucoup de liberté? ....

g Qui doit travailler à la maison le samedi et le dimanche? ....

Q Write a paragraph (about 50 words) about what your home life is like and what you think of it. Include an opinion about what you think teenage life should be like.

Young person in society

B Your future job

SPEAK

1 You're going to be asked about the jobs you'd like to do, so say these jobs out loud.

journaliste   employé(e) de banque   plombier   cadre   secrétaire   électricien(ne)   agent de police

2 Now you can use these jobs to talk about what you'd like to do. Choose as many jobs from the box as you like. Look at the examples below before you begin and try not to stick to the same example every time, but experiment to **make your answers as detailed as possible**.

3 Répondez à la question: Que pensez-vous faire comme métier plus tard? Answer the question: What do you think you'd like to do as a job later?

> Bien, plombier.

> Je voudrais être cadre.

> Je vais travailler comme secrétaire.

> Je vais aller à l'université pour faire mes études. Après ça je voudrais bien être journaliste pour un quotidien, parce que je m'intéresse beaucoup aux actualités et j'aime bien écrire.

Remember

Use conjunctions to make your sentences more interesting and detailed:
et (and), mais (but), ou (or), parce que/car (because), quand (when), cependant (however), donc (so, therefore).

4 Now you can build your answers up even more and really **impress the examiner**. The easiest way of doing that is by **giving your opinion and some extra details**. Say some longer sentences about jobs, using the ideas in the boxes below.

> J'aimerais bien devenir acteur/actrice parce que c'est un métier très intéressant et j'adore faire du théâtre.

> Je ne voudrais pas être médecin parce que c'est un métier trop fatigant et j'ai peur des hôpitaux!

teacher – stressful, dislike children

police officer – dangerous, dislike working at night

waiter/waitress – tiring, don't like cafés

hairdresser – interesting, like meeting people

mechanic – easy, love cars

vet – varied, love animals

PRACTICE

List three rules and three problems at this school.

> Notre directeur est très sévère et il y a une bonne discipline au lycée. Il est interdit de fumer et de prendre des drogues et on ne doit pas être impoli envers les profs. Il y a beaucoup plus de règles. Si on ne fait pas ses devoirs, par exemple, on sera mis en retenue. Malheureusement, il y a de la violence au lycée et de temps en temps les élèves attaquent les autres élèves dans la cour. Les autres grands problèmes, ce sont les graffiti et le vandalisme, mais ce sont des problèmes que l'on trouve partout dans la vie moderne.

> Make sure your writing is neat and clear – if the examiner can't read it, he/she can't tell if your answer's right.

Young person in society

Fashion

THE BARE BONES

➤ Make sure you learn items of clothing and colours to describe them (see page 45).

➤ If you have to write down six items, count what you have written to check there are six items – no fewer and no more.

A Clothes

Q Make a list of what you are wearing today. Add colours (see page 45) and descriptions: <u>un T-shirt; un T-shirt rouge; un grand T-shirt rouge.</u>

le manteau	coat	l'imperméable	raincoat
l'anorak	anorak	la veste	jacket
la chemise	shirt	la cravate	tie
le jean	jeans	le short	shorts
le jogging	tracksuit	le pantalon	trousers
le pyjama	pyjamas	le sweat-shirt	sweatshirt
le T-shirt	T-shirt	le pull	jumper
la jupe	skirt	la robe	dress
les baskets	trainers	les chaussettes	socks
les chaussures	shoes	le maillot de bain	swimming costume
la casquette	cap	le chapeau	hat

B Buying clothes

Est-ce que je peux vous aider?	Can I help you?
Je cherche (un manteau).	I'm looking for (a coat).
De quelle taille/pointure?	Which size/shoe size?
De quelle couleur?	Which colour?
En petite/en grande taille/en bleu.	Small/large/in blue.
En 38/en taille moyenne.	38/medium.
Est-ce que je peux l'essayer?	Can I try it on?
C'est trop grand/petit.	It's too big/small.
Ça coûte combien?	How much does it cost?
C'est trop cher/bon marché.	It's too expensive/cheap.
Je ne l'aime pas.	I don't like it.
Vous l'avez en plus grand?	Have you got a bigger one?
Je l'ai acheté aux soldes.	I bought it in the sales.
en laine/en cuir/en coton	woollen/leather/cotton

Remember
Add **–ci** (for 'this') and **–là** (for 'that') to the end of an item when you are comparing two things.

Grammar – this, that, these and those

masculine	le **ce**	J'aime **ce** pullover.	*I like this jumper.*
masculine	l' **cet**	J'ai acheté **cet** anorak.	*I bought this jacket.*
feminine	la **cette**	**Cette** jupe est jolie.	*This skirt is pretty.*
plural	les **ces**	**Ces** chaussures sont trop petites.	*These shoes are too small.*

Cet anorak-**là** est laid, mais **cet** anorak-**ci** est beau.   *That jacket is ugly, but this jacket is nice.*
J'aime **ces** chaussures-**ci** mais je déteste **ces** chaussures-**là**.   *I like these shoes, but I hate those shoes.*

Young person in society

C Describing clothes

WRITE

1 Sort out these anagrams. They're all items of clothing.

PUJE

CEHRAUUSSS

BORE

LAANTPON

ONBSOLU

MECESHI

2 Now include those clothes words in a sentence with two adjectives to describe each of them, as in the example below.

Exemple: C'est une **vieille** jupe **brune**.

| C'est ... | J'aime porter ... | Je déteste ... |

Grammar – adjectives

Most adjectives come after the noun, but **grand, petit, nouveau, vieux** come before.
Note their endings as well.

masculine singular:	un grand, petit, nouveau, vieux jean bleu
feminine singular:	une grand**e**, petit**e**, nouve**lle**, viei**lle** jupe bleu**e**
masculine plural:	deux grand**s**, petit**s**, nouve**aux**, vieux jeans bleu**s**
feminine plural:	deux grand**es**, petit**es**, nouve**lles**, viei**lles** jupes bleu**es**.

D At a clothes shop

1 Now you're going to put a dialogue in the right order. This time make sure that you **don't throw marks away** by writing your answer down wrongly – tick off each speech bubble once you've put it in order to check that:

- you've used all the speech bubbles and
- you haven't written down one of them twice by mistake.

READ

2 **Rangez les bulles. Put the speech bubbles in the correct order.**

a *Oui, il est beau. Je le prends.*

b *Non, il est trop cher.*

c *Taille trente.*

d *Bonjour. Je cherche un pullover.*

f *Bonjour, Madame. Vous désirez?*

e *Ce pullover est moins cher.*

h *Quelle taille?*

g *Vous aimez ce pullover ?*

What size does this person take?

PRACTICE

Write a list of six items of clothes you would take on holiday to France with you.

If you're asked to write a list of six words, such as a list of holiday clothes or a list of places in town – then do just that. You won't score extra marks for writing ten words and you can't score top marks unless you write the six words.

Young person in society

Remember
You'll hear each recording twice in the exam, so don't panic if you don't get all the answers on the first listening.

When you're doing the listening activities in this book, don't watch the Bitesize French video at the same time – just listen! You won't have time to watch the people as they talk and complete each activity. For each of the activities in this section, you'll need to:

- find the relevant part of the video
- read the task in this book that goes with the clip
- play the clip through once, listening carefully, and complete as much of the task as possible
- rewind the clip and play it again, filling in any gaps in your answers.
- check your answers at the back and make any corrections, then listen a third time to see if you can hear all the answers.

A Favourite school subjects

1 In this activity you listen to pupils answering the question: *Quelle est ta matière préférée?* You then have to tick the subjects mentioned. If you get a question like this in the exam, make sure you **read the words on the exam paper before you listen.**

2 Have a look at these words and try to work out what they'll sound like on the video.

la biologie l'italien le dessin l'anglais
les sciences naturelles les sciences économiques
la musique la gymnastique le français
les mathématiques le sport les sciences physiques

3 Now play the clip where the girl asks nine pupils: *Quelle est ta matière préférée?* and do the following activity.

4 Ecoutez et cochez les bons mots. Listen and tick the words (above) that you hear.

Q List five school subjects from the box, in English.

B Least favourite subjects

1 In the next clip the girl asks four pupils: *Quelle est la matière que tu aimes le moins?* Listen to the answers and do the following activity.

2 Ecoutez et cochez les bons mots. Listen and tick the words (above) that you hear.

Could you recognise all the words as you had read them beforehand?

C Julien's room

1 In the video, Julien shows you around his home – he uses some useful vocabulary for things you might have in your home. Look at the list below. Which of the things would you expect to find in the lounge (*le salon*) and which in Julien's room (*la chambre*)? Read the lists and check you understand the words before you listen.

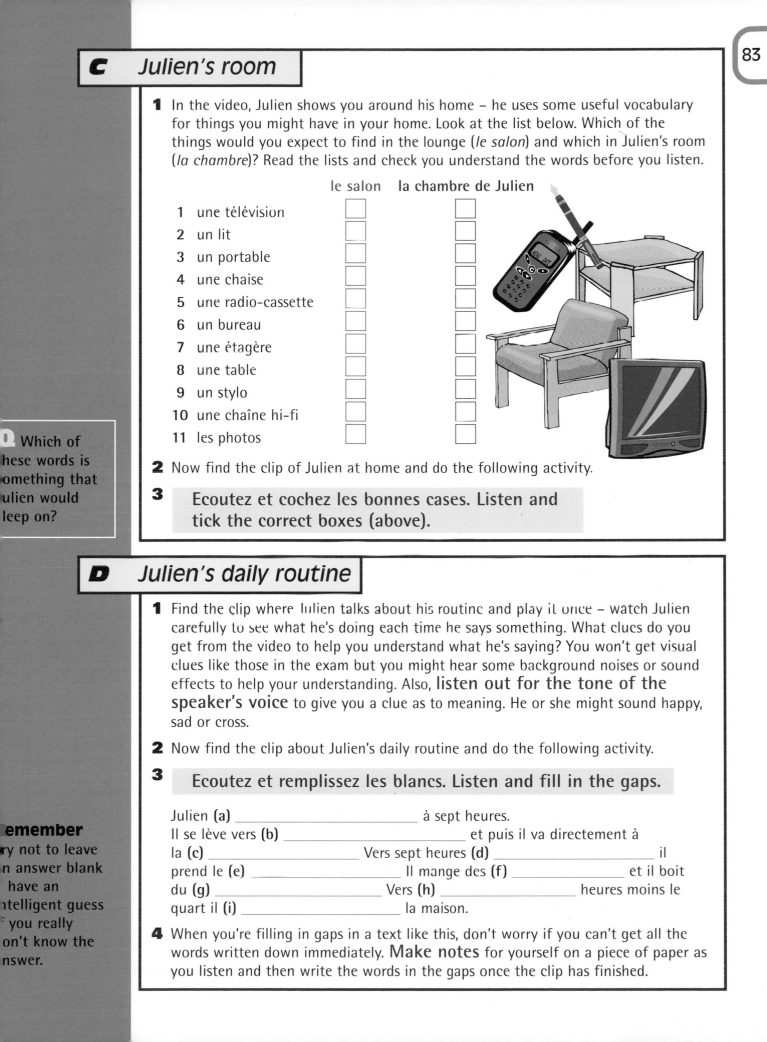

le salon   la chambre de Julien

1 une télévision	☐	☐
2 un lit	☐	☐
3 un portable	☐	☐
4 une chaise	☐	☐
5 une radio-cassette	☐	☐
6 un bureau	☐	☐
7 une étagère	☐	☐
8 une table	☐	☐
9 un stylo	☐	☐
10 une chaîne hi-fi	☐	☐
11 les photos	☐	☐

Q Which of these words is something that Julien would sleep on?

2 Now find the clip of Julien at home and do the following activity.

3 **Ecoutez et cochez les bonnes cases. Listen and tick the correct boxes (above).**

D Julien's daily routine

1 Find the clip where Julien talks about his routine and play it once – watch Julien carefully to see what he's doing each time he says something. What clues do you get from the video to help you understand what he's saying? You won't get visual clues like those in the exam but you might hear some background noises or sound effects to help your understanding. Also, **listen out for the tone of the speaker's voice** to give you a clue as to meaning. He or she might sound happy, sad or cross.

2 Now find the clip about Julien's daily routine and do the following activity.

3 **Ecoutez et remplissez les blancs. Listen and fill in the gaps.**

Julien **(a)** _____ à sept heures.
Il se lève vers **(b)** _____ et puis il va directement à
la **(c)** _____ Vers sept heures **(d)** _____ il
prend le **(e)** _____ Il mange des **(f)** _____ et il boit
du **(g)** _____ Vers **(h)** _____ heures moins le
quart il **(i)** _____ la maison.

Remember
Try not to leave an answer blank have an intelligent guess if you really don't know the answer.

4 When you're filling in gaps in a text like this, don't worry if you can't get all the words written down immediately. **Make notes** for yourself on a piece of paper as you listen and then write the words in the gaps once the clip has finished.

E Brothers and sisters

1 In the video nine teenagers are asked if they've got any brothers and sisters: *Tu as des frères ou des sœurs?* In the exam you might also hear several people giving information about themselves, which means that you're going to hear quite a few voices and a lot of information, so it's important that you're **prepared before the tape starts.**

2 The first thing to do is to **look at the task itself**, so you know what you've got to listen out for. What is this next task asking you to do?

3 Ecoutez et notez les réponses.

Tu as des frères ou des sœurs?

1 d	4	7
2	5	8
3	6	9

Remember
You might find it easier to note down 1f for un frère and 2s for deux sœurs while you're listening and then write the appropriate letter (a–e) afterwards.

4 Now check that:

- you understand the instruction
- you understand what the pictures mean
- you know where you've got to write the answer
- you know what sort of answer you've got to write (i.e. the letter a, b, c, d or e corresponding to the correct picture)
- you've got a pen or pencil ready to note down the answer.

5 Now find the clip on the video where the nine teenagers reply to the survey (*enquête*) about the number of brothers and sisters they've got, and do the activity above.

F Ages

1 Have a go at a similar activity now to see how well you can pick out details. Find the clip where eight people are giving the ages of their brothers and sisters and do this activity. **Remind yourself of the French numbers** first, as that's what you'll be listening out for.

Remember
Listen carefully to the number (un, deux, trois ...) of each speaker on the tape so you don't get lost.

2 Ecoutez et notez les âges. Listen and note the ages.

Les frères	Les sœurs
1 5	5
2	6
3	7
4	8

G Clémentine's family 🅗

1 When Clémentine introduces her family on the video, she gives lots of useful information about them. What sort of things do you need to say to introduce your family? Can you say four sentences to describe your family in French?

2 **Thinking of ideas yourself before you listen** to the tape is a good idea as you might then recognise some key words. For instance, if Clémentine is going to introduce her family, you can expect to hear words like *mère*, *père* and *frère* and maybe she'll use verbs like *travaille*, *habite* and *aime*. Do you know what those words mean?

3 Now find the clip where Clémentine is talking about her family and do the next activity.

4 **Ecoutez et remplissez les formulaires en français.**
Listen and fill in the forms in French.

Mère – nom:	[1]
Age:	[1]
Travail:	[1]
Adore:	[1]
Caractère:	[1]

Frère – nom:	[1]
Age:	[1]
Caractère:	[1]
Adore:	[1]
Aime le plus (animaux):	[1]
A combien?:	[1]

Père – travail:	[1]
Passe-temps (deux choses):	[2]
Caractère:	[1]

> The numbers in brackets – [1], [2] – show how many marks are available. To get two marks when there's a [2], you'll need to write down two details.

5 **Ecoutez encore une fois et répondez aux questions en français.**

1 La mère de Clémentine, elle travaille où? _____

2 Quel âge a-t-elle? _____

3 Qu'est-ce qu'elle boit comme une snob? _____

4 Qui est Emile? _____

🅗 5 Qu'est-ce qu'il a dans sa chambre? _____

6 Qui sont les meilleurs amis d'Emile? _____

7 Qui travaille à la poste? _____

8 A quelle heure va-t-il au travail? _____

9 Avec qui le père de Clémentine va au café? _____

10 Est-ce que Clémentine aime beaucoup son père? _____

Do you know what all the words on these forms mean?

Remember
Jot down rough notes while you listen and then write your answers neatly afterwards.

H Sports

1 Don't throw away marks in the exam by ticking the wrong box by mistake. Have a go at this activity and double-check that you've put your tick in the right place. It might help to **make a note in pencil** beside the names on the left-hand side of the grid and then find the picture afterwards and tick the box.

2 Find the clip on the video where seven teenagers are asked about the sports that they do: *Tu fais du sport?* Then look at the following activity and **run through the names for the sports depicted before you listen.**

3 Ecoutez et remplissez la grille. Listen and complete the grid.

	a	b	c	d	e	f	g	h	
1 MARIE									[1]
2 BERTRAND									[1]
3 PHILIPPE									[3]
4 ALEXANDRE									[1]
5 PATRICIA									[1]
6 NICOLAS									[3]
7 SABRINA									[2]

Remember
Always tick an answer, as even a guess at the end might score a mark, whereas a blank box won't score anything.

I Dijon

1 In the next clip, you'll hear people talking about Dijon and you then have to tick the statements that apply to the city. **Use your common sense** – you might know that Dijon is a big French city, so that can help you.

2 Ecoutez et cochez les bonnes cases.
Listen and tick the correct boxes.

Dijon

1 Il y a beaucoup de monuments. ☐
2 Pour les gens il n'y a rien à faire. ☐
3 Dijon est une ville très pauvre. ☐
4 On peut aller voir un opéra. ☐
5 Ici on trouve un Arc de Triomphe. ☐
6 A Dijon on peut faire des courses. ☐
7 Il n'y a pas de cafés au centre-ville. ☐
8 A Dijon on peut bien dîner. ☐

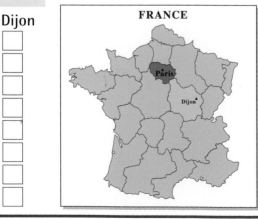

FRANCE

Paris

Dijon

Remember
You won't have an English translation of the activity instructions in the exam, so make sure you have learned them beforehand (see page 98).

J Jobs

1 Before you listen to the tape in the exam, it's a good idea to **think about a few words you might hear first**. Look at these English words for jobs and see if you know what French words you might hear on the video. Say them out loud or in your head.

train driver teacher banker doctor unemployed

2 Now find the clip where five people reply to the question: *Quel est votre travail?* and do the activity.

3 **Ecoutez et écrivez le métier de chaque personne. Listen and write down each person's job.**

1 La première femme est _____

2 La fille est _____

3 Le premier homme est _____

4 Le deuxième homme est _____

5 Le dernier homme est _____

Q Can you name four more jobs in French?

K Working hours

1 Play the clip where people are talking about their working hours and do the activity below. Remind yourself of how to tell the time in French first, by running through these clock faces and seeing if you can say them. For example: *a huit heures, huit heures trente* or *huit heures et demie, huit heures quinze* or *huit heures et quart, neuf heures.*

2 **Ecoutez et cochez la bonne heure. Listen and tick the correct time.**

1 08:00 ☐ 08:30 ☐ 08:15 ☐ 09:00 ☐

2 10:00 ☐ 08:30 ☐ 08:00 ☐ 09:00 ☐

3 07:00 ☐ 08:30 ☐ 18:00 ☐ 19:00 ☐

4 07:00 ☐ 17:00 ☐ 19:15 ☐ 20:00 ☐

5 16:25 ☐ 14:25 ☐ 15:20 ☐ 16:40 ☐

6 19:00 ☐ 13:00 ☐ 09:30 ☐ 20:00 ☐

7 22:10 ☐ 23:00 ☐ 22:00 ☐ 10:30 ☐

Remember
Check you know your French numbers before the exam – they're bound to come up somewhere!

You will have reading time before the tape is played in the exam, so use it wisely. Read through the questions and start thinking about the sorts of words and phrases that you might hear on the tape.

L **Adverts**

1 An important thing to remember in the exam, is **not to panic** – that won't get you anywhere! Activities like the next one might look scary but once you start them, you'll be able to cope. Just take a deep breath, relax and **tackle the activity bit by bit!**

2 Find the clips with the three adverts and do this activity.

3 Ecoutez et écrivez la bonne lettre.
Listen and write the correct letter.

1 La première publicité, c'est pour

a quelque chose à manger

b quelque chose à boire

c quelque chose à porter. ☐

2 La deuxième publicité, c'est pour

a une école

b une boisson

c quelque chose de sucré. ☐

3 Dans ce produit, il y a

a du fromage

b du poisson

c du chocolat. ☐

4 La troisième publicité, c'est pour

a la crème

b le dentifrice

c les dentistes. ☐

5 On peut

a boire ce produit

b voir et sentir ce produit

c jouer avec ce produit. ☐

Q Can you find at least four verbs in these questions? What do they mean?

PRACTICE

When you've got a spare moment, put the French Bitesize video on and play a clip that you find particularly interesting – or one that covers the topic area you're revising at the time. Listen and watch the clip through once and note down any key words you'd like to learn. Then rewind the tape and play the clip again – but this time with the volume turned right down. Pause the tape every so often and say a sentence or phrase to describe what you can see or what's happening. Then carry on like this, pausing and speaking and then continuing.

You can then watch the clip again at the end with the volume turned up and see how much you remembered or compare the things that you said with the actual French speakers.

M Countries

1 In the next activity you're going to **tick a grid as you listen**. This can be a bit tricky as, if you miss a number by mistake and think that you're listening to number 3 when in fact it's already number 4, then all your answers will be wrong, even if you understand the French – you'd be ticking on the wrong line. You can avoid this by **putting a blank piece of paper on the grid** and each time the tape gives a number (*un, deux* etc.) **pull the paper down a line and tick on that line**. Try it with this activity – just pull the paper down each time you hear a new voice.

2 Now find the clip where nine people answer the survey question: *D'où venez-vous?* and do the activity.

3 Ecoutez et cochez la grille. Listen and tick the grid.

	Belgium	Italy	England	Germany	Canada	France	Switzerland
1							
2							
3							
4							
5							
6							
7							
8							
9							

Remember
Make sure you ck the corect pace on a grid take care not o muddle the nes.

N Hotel Canelle

1 In the next activity you're going to fill in a form as you listen. **Check you understand all the headings on it first** and know what sort of words you've got to write in the spaces. Then find the clip where Manuel talks about Hôtel Canelle and do the activity.

2 Ecoutez et remplissez le formulaire. Listen and complete the form.

Look out for words like <u>3 choses</u> on the exam paper – this means that you've got to note down three items to gain full marks.

Hôtel Canelle

1 Manuel: âge –   2 Son père est:

3 Combien de chambres:

4 l'hôtel se trouve:

5 Pour le petit déjeuner [3 choses]:

6 Facilités à l'hôtel [4 choses]:

Which meal mentioned on his form?

Listening

You need the clip on the Bitesize video that takes place in Marks & Spencer for this activity.

On fait des courses chez Marks & Spencer. Ecoutez et trouvez la bonne réponse. Ecrivez la bonne lettre.

1 La première dame a acheté:

A un short pour la fête

B un short pour l'été

C un short pour son enfant. **B** *[1]*

5 La robe de la dame est:

A marron

B rouge

C bleue. ☐ *[1]*

2 La deuxième dame a acheté:

A un jean et une chemise

B deux jeans et une robe

C un jean pour son mari. ☐ *[1]*

6 L'homme a acheté:

A des chaussures

B des chaussettes

C un pantalon. ☐ *[1]*

3 La jeune fille a acheté:

A une jupe d'été

B une chemise d'été

C une robe d'été. ☐ *[1]*

7 Le dernier homme a acheté:

A un pullover blanc

B un pullover vert

C un pullover rouge. ☐ *[1]*

4 La casquette de sa copine:

A a coûté 96 francs

B a coûté 67 francs

C a coûté 69 francs. ☐ *[1]*

8 Le pullover:

A a coûté 249 francs

B a coûté 49 francs

C a coûté 349 francs. ☐ *[1]*

Now play the clip again and listen through for a second time.

A What skills do I need?

You are expected to:

1 use your preparation time to read and understand the instruction and any questions/sentences on the paper.

2 listen to the tape carefully first time through.

3 write the correct letter for each answer clearly in the box.

4 listen to the tape a second time and check or fill in any missing answers.

B Extra tips

1 Always look at any example answer you are given to see what you are expected to do.

2 Read the questions on the exam paper before you listen so that you get an idea about what you might hear – you will be given time to do this.

3 Read every answer through very carefully on multiple choice activities. Sometimes they might be very similar, like 1A and 1B here, so it's important that you don't confuse them and write down the wrong letter in the box.

4 Check all your answers when the tape is played for the second time – have you really written down the right answer?

5 Don't lose your way while you're listening and get left behind. If you don't know the answer, then don't stop, just miss the question out and carry on with the next ones. You can always come back to any missing answers on your second listening.

6 Never leave a tick box blank – always write an answer, as even a guess at the end might score a mark, whereas a blank box won't score anything.

C Remember

1 If you change your mind about an answer on a second listening, cross out the wrong answer and write your changed answer clearly – you won't score marks if the examiner can't make out what you've written.

2 You can always scribble notes on the paper while you're listening and then write the letter in the box after the recording.

3 Work out a system of note-taking before you go into the exam. So, for instance, if you hear *un pullover vert*, you could just note *pull vert*. You can always go back to your notes and write them as proper answers after the tape has finished, if necessary.

4 If you have to answer questions on a passage in French or English, don't write full sentences as just single words or short phrase answers will probably do.

5 Look out for any questions which carry two or more marks (usually shown in brackets by the question) and make sure you give enough details in your answer to get full marks.

6 Listen out for the tone of the speaker's voice to help give you a clue as to meaning. He or she might sound happy, sad, angry or cross.

D Model answers

1B, 2A, 3C, 4C, 5C, 6A, 7B, 8A

Speaking

---

1 Foundation role play: At the station

You are at a train station. Your teacher will speak first.

[teacher: Bonjour.]

- ask for two single tickets to Cannes

[teacher: Les voilà.]

- ask how much it costs

[teacher: Cinquante euros vingt, s'il vous plaît.]

- ask when the next train leaves

[teacher: A dix heures trente-deux.]

- ask which platform the train leaves from

[teacher: Quai numéro sept.]

- ask if you have to change trains

[teacher: Non, le train est direct.]

---

2 Higher role play: Jobs

You are talking about jobs with your French penfriend. Your teacher will play the part of your penfriend and will speak first.

[teacher: Tu as un petit boulot?]

- petit boulot et l'argent

[teacher: Pourquoi fais-tu ça?]

- pourquoi faire ça?

[teacher: Quand fais-tu ce travail?]

- les heures du travail

[teacher: Tu fais ça depuis longtemps?]

- depuis quand?

---

3 General conversation: Free time

1 Qu'est-ce que vous aimez faire dans votre temps libre?

2 Vous aimez faire du sport?

3 Où avez-vous passé les dernières vacances?

4 Comment y êtes-vous allé?

5 C'était comment le voyage?

6 Qu'est-ce que vous avez fait là-bas?

A What skills do I need?

You are expected to:

1 listen to the examiner's questions for the **role play** and answer according to the information given on the cue card – either words or pictures.

2 prepare a **presentation** on a topic beforehand to talk about (see pages 123–128 – last-minute learner section – for ideas to start you off).

3 be prepared to answer **general conversation questions** on a topic.

B Extra tips

1 Always speak clearly and slowly – your exam will be recorded onto tape, so mumbles and slurred speech won't sound good to the examiner.

2 Try to speak confidently with a good French pronunciation.

3 Always try to be polite in role plays by using: *Bonjour. Merci bien. S'il vous plaît. Au revoir.*

4 If you can't understand what the examiner is saying, ask politely: *Comment?* (Pardon?) or *Pardon, mais je ne comprends pas.* (Sorry, but I don't understand.) or *Pouvez-vous répéter ça, s'il vous plaît?* (Can you repeat that, please?).

5 Give as many details in answer to questions as you can – try to avoid giving just one-word answers.

C Remember

1 You'll need to use different tenses (present, past and future) to get top marks and you'll also need to give your opinion whenever possible.

2 Always address the examiner as *vous* unless told to do otherwise.

3 If you can't think of the actual word you want, then use another word instead. For example, if you can't remember how to say 'I was born in Spain' then change it to 'I come from Spain': *Je viens d'Espagne.*

4 If you're running out of things to say, then give your opinion: *J'aime/adore ça. Je trouve ça marrant/ennuyeux …*

5 If you realise you've said something wrong, don't panic – just say: *Ah, excusez-moi,* and correct yourself.

D Model answers

1 Foundation role play: At the station

- Bonjour. Deux allers simples pour Cannes, s'il vous plaît.
- Ça coûte combien?
- Merci. A quelle heure part le prochain train?
- Merci bien. Et le train part de quel quai?
- Bon. Est-ce qu'il faut changer?

2 Higher role play: Jobs

- Oui, je travaille dans un café et je gagne cinq euros de l'heure.
- Parce que je voudrais faire des économies pour acheter un VTT et aussi j'aime travailler avec des gens au café. Je trouve le boulot très très intéressant.
- Je travaille le samedi de neuf heures du matin jusqu'à quatre heures de l'après-midi – c'est bien fatigant!
- Non, j'ai commencé le travail l'année dernière mais j'espère travailler ici quelques années.

3 General conversation: Free time

1 J'aime aller aux boums, écouter de la musique et faire la cuisine. Je n'aime pas chanter ou jouer du piano.

2 Oui, j'aime faire de la natation et jouer au foot et au basket. J'adore le basket surtout!

3 Je suis allé(e) en Italie avec ma famille. Nous sommes restés dans un petit hôtel au bord de la mer. C'était super.

4 On y est allé(e)s en voiture. Ma mère a conduit parce que mon père s'est cassé la jambe.

5 Le voyage était pénible parce qu'il a duré trop longtemps. Je l'ai trouvé très ennuyeux.

6 J'ai beaucoup nagé dans la mer et je me suis bien bronzé(e) sur la plage parce qu'il faisait soleil tous les jours.

Reading

Two reading activities for you to try on the same passage.

1 Qui mentionne des choses A–E? Lisez les textes, regardez les images et écrivez le nom.

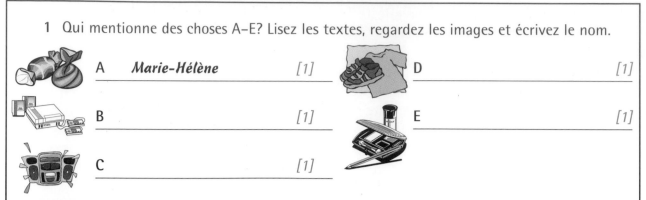

A *Marie-Hélène* [1]

B _____ [1]

C _____ [1]

D _____ [1]

E _____ [1]

Pascal – Mes parents me donnent dix euros par semaine et je trouve ça pas mal. En ce moment, je fais des économies parce que je voudrais bien acheter une nouvelle chaîne-stéréo.

Baudouin – Moi, j'ai un petit boulot au café le week-end et je gagne 4,50 euros de l'heure. Je trouve le travail intéressant parce que j'aime bien parler aux gens et le patron est très sympa. J'aime acheter des vêtements et des magazines avec mon argent.

Mireille – Je ne reçois pas d'argent de poche parce que j'ai un petit emploi. Je fais du babysitting tous les vendredis pour nos voisins. Je travaille de dix-sept heures jusqu'à vingt-deux heures et je trouve ça bien fatigant. Mais je gagne huit euros de l'heure et ça me plaît beaucoup! J'achète des CDs et du maquillage avec mon argent.

Marie-Hélène – *Je reçois vingt euros par mois de mon père et dix euros par mois de ma mère. J'achète des bonbons et des jeux-vidéos avec ça. J'aimerais bien trouver un petit emploi, mais j'habite dans un petit village à la campagne, et ici il n'y a pas d'emplois pour les ados.*

2 Répondez aux questions **en français**.

a Qui travaille le samedi?   *Baudouin* [1]

b Où habite Marie-Hélène? _____ [1]

c Combien d'argent de poche reçoit Pascal? _____ [1]

d Quand travaille Mireille? _____ [1]

e Qu'est-ce que Pascal fait avec son argent de poche? _____ [1]

f Pourquoi Marie-Hélène n'a pas de travail? _____ [1]

g Pourquoi Baudouin aime-t-il travailler au café? _____ [2]

_____

A What skills do I need?

You are expected to:

1 understand the instructions for the activity (see page 98 for a list of instructions).

2 read the passage and answer accordingly – following any example answer provided.

B Extra tips

1 If you're not sure of an answer, don't spend ages puzzling over it – leave it and come back to it if there's time at the end of the exam.

2 Read any small question words carefully so you don't misunderstand them:
Où? (Where?)
Qui? (Who?)
Quand? (When?)
Comment? (How?)
Combien? (How many?)
Pourquoi? (Why?)
Qu'est-ce que ...? (What).

3 Read the instruction for each task very carefully to make sure that you're answering in the correct way. Don't assume that you know what the task is before you've read the instruction thoroughly.

4 If the exercise says tick four things, do just that – don't tick five or six.

5 You can scribble over the exam paper and cross things out if you want to – it's not like a textbook in class.

6 Try to leave time to go over your answers at the end of the exam to double-check them.

C Remember

1 If it is a lengthy reading passage, read it through once to get the gist of it before working on the actual questions.

2 Look out for how many marks each question has – if there is more than one mark, then you'll need to give more than one bit of information in your answer.

3 Don't spend all your time on the first reading activity and not have time to finish the exam paper.

4 If the questions on the paper are in French, answer in French and if they are in English, answer in English, unless the paper tells you differently.

5 Watch out for the tenses in the reading passages and answer accordingly. You'll come across present, past and future tenses, so go into the exam prepared to recognise these.

6 In the Higher paper, there will be some unfamiliar vocabulary that you'll have to cope with, but don't panic. Some words look like their English equivalent – a picture on the paper might help you. The rest of the text or the exercise questions might help you understand it or you might even be able to complete the exercise without knowing it.

D Model answers

1 A Marie-Hélène B Marie-Hélène C Pascal D Baudouin E Mireille

2 a Baudouin b un petit village c dix euros par semaine d tous les vendredis de 17:00–22:00 heures e fait des économies f pas d'emplois pour les ados dans le village g aime parler aux gens/le patron est très sympa

Writing

---

1 Add six items of fruit or vegetables to this list.

le chou   **la pomme**   **les cerises**

_____   _____   _____

_____   _____   _____   [6]

---

2 Write an email to your French friend about your weekend activities.
Write about 40 words and give the following information:

- day/activity

- who with?

- TV/music   [10]

Higher writing

Choisissez A ou B ci-dessous et écrivez 100–120 mots.

A Ecrivez une lettre à votre correspondant(e) pour parler de votre boulot.

- où travaillez-vous? qu'est-ce que vous faites?

- l'argent que vous avez gagné – acheter? faire des économies?

- expliquez pourquoi le travail est idéal/terrible

- une chose intéressante qui s'est passée la semaine dernière.

B Vous voulez faire un stage dans une compagnie française. Ecrivez un texte et parlez:

- de vous et de vos qualités personnelles

- de vos passe-temps

- de vos études au collège

- des emplois que vous avez déjà eus.

Expliquez pourquoi vous voulez faire ce stage.   [20]

Grammar – four tenses

Present tense	Perfect tense	Imperfect tense	Future tense
je suis	j'ai été	j'étais	je serai (je vais être)
j'ai	j'ai eu	j'avais	j'aurai (je vais avoir)
je fais	j'ai fait	je faisais	je ferai (je vais faire)
je vais	je suis allé(e)	j'allais	j'irai (je vais aller)

A What skills do I need?

You are expected to:

1 follow the instruction for the activity and stick to what you are asked to do.

2 pace yourself so you are able to answer all the questions in the allocated time.

B Extra tips

1 Check that your handwriting is legible and that your written work makes sense.

2 After you've completed your tasks, check your spelling, accents and grammar (adjective agreements, tenses, pronouns etc.).

3 If you get a choice of writing tasks and you choose to answer A, stick with it. Don't change your mind halfway through and try to answer B instead as you'll probably run out of time.

C Remember

1 If you've got 120 words to write, think of six headings to do with the topic area or use those provided on the paper and write brief notes/key words under each. Then write your text out in full, padding your notes out to about twenty words on each heading.

2 If the question asks for specific information, work your way through the headings one by one, ticking them off as you go.

3 If you're struggling to know what to write, include as many opinion phrases as you can (in the present and past tense): *... est/était formidable/génial. Je trouve/j'ai trouvé ... cool/super/ affreux/dangereux/intéressant. ... me plaît beaucoup/... m'a beaucoup plu.*

4 Always add details of time and place to make your writing more interesting: *Ça s'est passé le week-end dernier. Je travaillais à la banque entre huit et quatre heures – c'était fatigant.*

D Model answers

1 Look at page 65 for vocabulary.

2 ```
Cher Patrick,
Le samedi je retrouve mes copains au
centre-ville. J'adore faire ça – c'est
marrant. Le dimanche je joue au tennis
au centre sportif avec mon père. Je
trouve ça fatigant. Le soir je regarde
la télé dans le salon.

A bientôt   Paul
```

3 Make sure that in either answer you have:
- written about all the points mentioned
- included past, present and future tenses in your text.
- included your opinion, where possible
- written the letter properly: town and date on right-hand side, *Cher* + boy's name, *Chère* + girl's name.

## Coursework option

1 If you've chosen to do coursework instead of the written exam, make sure the work you submit is neatly presented (typed up on a computer if permitted) and grammatically correct.

2 Before you submit your work, check that all parts of the task have been completed.

3 While writing, try to include plenty of descriptions by using adjectives.

4 Give an opinion on the topic wherever possible: *A mon avis . . .; Je trouve . . .*

5 Add some reasons in your text by lengthening sentences to include *parce que . . .*

6 Make sure that your sentences are varied in style. Don't just write short sentences but make them longer by using conjunctions – *mais, et, ou, quand.*

7 Make sure you've included sentences in the past tense as well as the present. Try to add what will happen in the future too – this will help you to get the top grades.
```

Instructions

These are the main instructions (rubrics) that you may see at the beginning of exercises in the GCSE exam. They tell you what you are expected to do for each question. In your exam, instructions may be given in the **vous** or **tu** form - check with your teacher which one your exam board uses.

Choisissez (Choisis) la bonne réponse dans la liste.	*Choose the correct answer from the list.*
Cochez (Coche) la bonne phrase.	*Tick the correct sentence.*
Cochez (Coche) la bonne case.	*Tick the correct box.*
Complétez (Complète) (les phrases) en français.	*Complete (the sentences) in French.*
Décrivez (Décris) . . .	*Describe . . .*
Ecoutez (Ecoute) . . .	*Listen . . .*
Ecrivez (Ecris) environ 100 mots.	*Write about 100 words.*
Ecrivez (Ecris) une phrase.	*Write a sentence.*
Ecrivez (Ecris) les détails.	*Write the details.*
Ecrivez (Ecris) la bonne lettre.	*Write the correct letter.*
Ecrivez (Ecris) P (positif), N (négatif) ou P+N (positif et négatif).	*Write P (positive), N (negative) or P+N (positive and negative).*
Ecrivez (Ecris) les lettres (A, B, C ou D) dans le bon ordre.	*Write the letters (A, B, C or D) in the right order.*
Ecrivez votre (Ecris ton) avis avec vos (tes) raisons.	*Write your opinion with your reasons.*
Expliquez (Explique) . . .	*Explain . . .*
Faites (Fais) correspondre les images aux mots.	*Match the pictures to the words.*
Faites (Fais) une liste (de vêtements) en français.	*Write a list (of clothes) in French.*
Faites (Fais) un résumé.	*Write a summary.*
Identifiez (Identifie) les phrases vraies.	*Identify the true sentences.*

Instructions *Continued*

Indiquez (Indique) si les phrases sont vraies (V) ou fausses (F) ou si on ne ou si on ne sait pas.	*Indicate whether the sentences are true (V), false (F) or if you can't tell.*
Lisez (Lis) le texte.	*Read the text.*
Lisez (Lis) la letter.	*Read the letter.*
Lisez (Lis) l'exemple.	*Read the example.*
Lisez (Lis) les phrases suivantes.	*Read the following sentences.*
Mettez (Mets) (les illustrations) dans le bon ordre.	*Put (the pictures) in the right order.*
Mentionnez (Mentionne) (trois détails).	*Mention (three details).*
Notez (Note) . . .	*Note . . .*
Regardez (Regarde) cette publicité.	*Look at this advert.*
Regardez (Regarde) ces illustrations.	*Look at these pictures.*
Remplissez (Remplis) la grille en français/anglais.	*Fill in the grid in French/English.*
Répondez (Réponds) aux questions en français.	*Answer the questions in French.*
Soulignez (Souligne) . . .	*Underline . . .*
Traduisez (Traduis) ces phrases en français.	*Translate the sentences into French.*
Trouvez (Trouve) la bonne réponse.	*Find the correct answer.*
Utilisez (Utilise) les mots dans la liste ci-dessous.	*Use the words in the list below.*
Qu'est-ce que cela veut dire?	*What does that mean?*

Topic checker

- Go through these questions after you've revised a group of topics, putting a tick if you know the answer and a cross if you don't – you can check your answers on the page references given.
- Try these questions again the next time you revise ... until you've got a column that's all ticks! Then you'll know you can be confident.

My world

All about me

Can you give your name and age?	(p.8)	☐ ☐ ☐
Can you count to sixty?	(p.8)	☐ ☐ ☐
Can you name the twelve months of the year?	(p.8)	☐ ☐ ☐
Can you name six nationalities?	(p.8)	☐ ☐ ☐
Can you describe your hair and eyes?	(p.9)	☐ ☐ ☐
Can you name six pets?	(p.9)	☐ ☐ ☐
Can you say the French alphabet?	(p.9)	☐ ☐ ☐
Can you name five male and five female family members?	(p.12)	☐ ☐ ☐
Can you name four positive and four negative characteristics?	(p.12)	☐ ☐ ☐
Can you name three special occasions in the year?	(p.13)	☐ ☐ ☐

All about my house

Can you name seven rooms in a house?	(p.16)	☐ ☐ ☐
Can you name eight pieces of furniture?	(p.16)	☐ ☐ ☐
Can you say what sort of house you live in?	(p.16)	☐ ☐ ☐
Can you say that you share your room with your sister?	(p.16)	☐ ☐ ☐
Can you name four places you might live?	(p.17)	☐ ☐ ☐
Can you say how many inhabitants there are in your town/village?	(p.17)	☐ ☐ ☐

School

Can you name ten school subjects?	(p.20)	☐ ☐ ☐
Can you say one subject that you don't like and why not?	(p.20)	☐ ☐ ☐
Can you say one subject you like and why?	(p.20)	☐ ☐ ☐
Can you name two types of school?	(p.20)	☐ ☐ ☐
Can you name four rooms in a school?	(p.20)	☐ ☐ ☐
Can you describe your uniform?	(p.20)	☐ ☐ ☐

The 12-hour clock

Can you say it's two/four o'clock?	(p.21)	☐ ☐ ☐
Can you say it's quarter past two?	(p.21)	☐ ☐ ☐
Can you say it's half past two?	(p.21)	☐ ☐ ☐
Can you say it's ten/five to three?	(p.21)	☐ ☐ ☐
Can you say it's midnight/midday?	(p.21)	☐ ☐ ☐
Can you ask 'what's the time?'	(p.21)	☐ ☐ ☐

Daily routine

Can you give four sentences about your daily routine?	(p.21)	☐ ☐ ☐
Can you say when the first school lesson starts?	(p.21)	☐ ☐ ☐

Holiday time and travel

In town

Can you name six things there are in your town?	(p.24)	☐ ☐ ☐
Can you name eight shops?	(p.24)	☐ ☐ ☐
Can you ask where the toilets and the cinema are?	(p.25)	☐ ☐ ☐
Can you say it's on the left/right?	(p.25)	☐ ☐ ☐
Can you tell someone to take the first road on the right?	(p.25)	☐ ☐ ☐
Can you tell someone to go straight ahead?	(p.25)	☐ ☐ ☐
Can you tell a stranger to cross the bridge/square?	(p.25)	☐ ☐ ☐

Holiday time and travel continued

Can you say it's between the station and the post office?	(p.25)	☐ ☐ ☐
Can you tell a stranger to take the second road on the left?	(p.25)	☐ ☐ ☐
Can you say it's behind the church?	(p.25)	☐ ☐ ☐

The 24-hr clock

Can you say these times in French: 01:10, 10:15, 13:40, 18:00, 22:30?	(p.28)	☐ ☐ ☐

Buying a train ticket

Can you ask for a single ticket to Calais?	(p.28)	☐ ☐ ☐
Can you ask for a return ticket to Dieppe?	(p.28)	☐ ☐ ☐
Can you ask for non-smoking in standard class?	(p.28)	☐ ☐ ☐
Can you ask which platform the train leaves from?	(p.28)	☐ ☐ ☐
Can you ask what time the train leaves/arrives?	(p.28)	☐ ☐ ☐
Can you say that the train is late?	(p.28)	☐ ☐ ☐

Forms of transport

Can you say you go on foot?	(p.29)	☐ ☐ ☐
Can you say you go by bus/coach?	(p.29)	☐ ☐ ☐
Can you say you go by bike?	(p.29)	☐ ☐ ☐
Can you say you go by car/taxi?	(p.29)	☐ ☐ ☐
Can you say you go by plane/lorry?	(p.29)	☐ ☐ ☐
Can you say you go by train/underground?	(p.29)	☐ ☐ ☐

Countries

Can you name ten countries?	(p.32)	☐ ☐ ☐
Can you say the nationalities as well?	(p.32)	☐ ☐ ☐

A past holiday

Can you say you went to Paris?	(p.32)	☐ ☐ ☐
Can you say you went by train?	(p.32)	☐ ☐ ☐

Can you say you spent a week in France?	(p.33)	☐	☐	☐
Can you say you went abroad last year?	(p.33)	☐	☐	☐
Can you say you went to the mountains/seaside?	(p.33)	☐	☐	☐
Can you say you stayed at a campsite?	(p.33)	☐	☐	☐
Can you say the weather was good/bad?	(p.33)	☐	☐	☐
Can you name two things you did on holiday?	(p.33)	☐	☐	☐

Youth hostel

How do you say 'youth hostel', 'dormitory' and 'bed' in French?	(p.36)	☐	☐	☐
Can you ask to hire a mountain bike?	(p.36)	☐	☐	☐

Campsite

Can you name four things to take on a camping holiday?	(p.36)	☐	☐	☐
Can you name three facilities at a campsite?	(p.36)	☐	☐	☐
Can you ask how much it costs?	(p.36)	☐	☐	☐

Staying with a penfriend

Can you say four greetings you might hear on a visit to someone?	(p.37)	☐	☐	☐
How do you say 'pleased to meet you'?	(p.37)	☐	☐	☐
Can you say that you haven't got any toothpaste/soap?	(p.37)	☐	☐	☐
Can you say one thing you might say at the end of a visit to a penfriend?	(p.37)	☐	☐	☐

Booking into a hotel

Can you ask if there are any rooms free?	(p.40)	☐	☐	☐
Can you ask for a single/double room?	(p.40)	☐	☐	☐
Can you say it's for two nights/people?	(p.40)	☐	☐	☐
Can you ask for a room with a bath or a shower?	(p.40)	☐	☐	☐
Can you name five facilities in a hotel?	(p.40)	☐	☐	☐

The weather

Can you name four different weather conditions?	(p.41)	☐	☐	☐
Can you say it was nice or bad?	(p.41)	☐	☐	☐
Can you say it's going to rain?	(p.41)	☐	☐	☐
Can you name the four seasons of the year?	(p.41)	☐	☐	☐

Telephone

Can you ask to talk to somebody on the phone?	(p.44)	☐	☐	☐
Can you ask to leave a message?	(p.44)	☐	☐	☐
Can you give your phone number?	(p.44)	☐	☐	☐

Bank

Can you say you'd like to change a traveller's cheque?	(p.44)	☐	☐	☐
Can you say you'd like to change pounds sterling to euros?	(p.44)	☐	☐	☐

Post

Can you ask to send a letter to France?	(p.44)	☐	☐	☐
Can you ask for three two-euro stamps?	(p.44)	☐	☐	☐
Can you ask for four stamps for England?	(p.44)	☐	☐	☐

Reporting a loss

Can you ask for the lost property office?	(p.45)	☐	☐	☐
Can you name three things that you have lost?	(p.45)	☐	☐	☐
Can you say somebody has stolen your camera/purse?	(p.45)	☐	☐	☐
Can you name eight colours?	(p.45)	☐	☐	☐

Reporting an accident

Can you say you were driving quickly/too fast?	(p.45)	☐	☐	☐
Can you say the accident happened on the A6 motorway?	(p.45)	☐	☐	☐
Can you say two people were killed?	(p.45)	☐	☐	☐
Can you call for help?	(p.45)	☐	☐	☐

Work and lifestyle

Hobbies				
Can you name six (non-sporting) hobbies?	(p.48)	☐	☐	☐
Can you say you love doing something?	(p.48)	☐	☐	☐
Can you say you hate doing something?	(p.48)	☐	☐	☐
Can you name five sports?	(p.48)	☐	☐	☐
How often				
Can you name the seven days of the week?	(p.49)	☐	☐	☐
Can you say you do something often/each weekend/now and again?	(p.49)	☐	☐	☐
Can you say you are sporty/not sporty?	(p.49)	☐	☐	☐
Media				
Can you name four types of TV programmes?	(p.52)	☐	☐	☐
Can you say what your favourite programme is?	(p.52)	☐	☐	☐
Can you say who your favourite singer/group is?	(p.52)	☐	☐	☐
Can you say which films you love?	(p.52)	☐	☐	☐
Can you say which films you dislike?	(p.52)	☐	☐	☐
Can you say you saw an interesting/boring play?	(p.52)	☐	☐	☐
Can you say you read a book about a family and it took place in Italy?	(p.52)	☐	☐	☐
Inviting somebody out				
Can you ask someone if they are free this weekend?	(p.53)	☐	☐	☐
Can you invite someone to two different events?	(p.53)	☐	☐	☐
Can you say you are not free?	(p.53)	☐	☐	☐
Can you ask when and where you will meet?	(p.53)	☐	☐	☐

Work and lifestyle continued

Jobs

Can you name ten jobs (male and female if possible)?	(p.56)	☐	☐	☐
Can you say your father works as a doctor?	(p.56)	☐	☐	☐
Can you say a family member is unemployed?	(p.56)	☐	☐	☐
Can you name four places you might work?	(p.56)	☐	☐	☐

Helping at home

Can you name five household chores?	(p.60)	☐	☐	☐
Can you say you cook breakfast/lunch/dinner?	(p.60)	☐	☐	☐
Can you give three time expressions for when you help?	(p.60)	☐	☐	☐

Work experience

Can you name four things you did on an office work experience?	(p.60)	☐	☐	☐

Part-time work and pocket money

Can you say two part-time jobs you do?	(p.61)	☐	☐	☐
Can you say when you start and finish?	(p.61)	☐	☐	☐
Can you say you earn six euros an hour?	(p.61)	☐	☐	☐
Can you say you're saving?	(p.61)	☐	☐	☐
Can you say your parents give you eight euros a week?	(p.61)	☐	☐	☐

Illness and parts of the body

Can you name seven things that might be wrong with you?	(p.64)	☐	☐	☐
Can you say you're tired?	(p.64)	☐	☐	☐
Can you name ten parts of the body?	(p.64)	☐	☐	☐

Fruit and vegetables

Can you name eight fruit varieties?	(p.65)	☐	☐	☐
Can you name six vegetable varieties?	(p.65)	☐	☐	☐

Higher numbers

Can you count from 60 to 100?	(p.65)	☐ ☐ ☐
Can you say 200, 1000 and 2000?	(p.65)	☐ ☐ ☐

Quantities

Can you ask for a box of something?	(p.65)	☐ ☐ ☐
Can you ask for 500 grammes of apples?	(p.65)	☐ ☐ ☐

Food and drink

Can you name nine items of food?	(p.68)	☐ ☐ ☐
Can you name three things you like eating?	(p.68)	☐ ☐ ☐
Can you name two things you dislike eating?	(p.68)	☐ ☐ ☐
Can you name four drinks?	(p.68)	☐ ☐ ☐

At a restaurant

Can you ask for a table for two people?	(p.68)	☐ ☐ ☐
Can you ask for Saturday night at 8pm?	(p.68)	☐ ☐ ☐
How do you call the waiter/waitress over in a restaurant?	(p.69)	☐ ☐ ☐
Can you say what you'd like for starters?	(p.69)	☐ ☐ ☐
Can you say you'd like some red/white wine?	(p.69)	☐ ☐ ☐
Can you ask for the bill?	(p.69)	☐ ☐ ☐

Restaurant complaints

Can you say you haven't got a knife?	(p.69)	☐ ☐ ☐
Can you say the soup is cold?	(p.69)	☐ ☐ ☐
Can you say there's too much pepper/salt?	(p.69)	☐ ☐ ☐
Can you say you had to wait an hour for your pizza?	(p.69)	☐ ☐ ☐

Young person in society

The environment

Can you name three environmental problems?	(p.72)	☐ ☐ ☐
Can you name three things you do to protect the environment?	(p.72)	☐ ☐ ☐

Smoking, alcohol and drugs

Can you say whether you smoke or not?	(p.72)	☐ ☐ ☐
Can you say you smoke ten cigarettes a day?	(p.72)	☐ ☐ ☐
Can you say whether you drink alcohol or not?	(p.73)	☐ ☐ ☐
Can you say you want to give up drinking?	(p.73)	☐ ☐ ☐
Can you say you don't take any drugs?	(p.73)	☐ ☐ ☐
Can you say you find something dangerous?	(p.73)	☐ ☐ ☐

Future plans

Can you say you're going into the sixth form next year?	(p.76)	☐ ☐ ☐
Can you say you're going to leave school?	(p.76)	☐ ☐ ☐
Can you say you're going to do an apprenticeship?	(p.76)	☐ ☐ ☐
Can you say you hope to study abroad?	(p.76)	☐ ☐ ☐
Can you say you'll look for a well-paid job?	(p.76)	☐ ☐ ☐
Can you say where you'd like to work?	(p.76)	☐ ☐ ☐

Adolescence

Can you name four teenage problems?	(p.76)	☐ ☐ ☐
Can you say four things about life at home?	(p.76)	☐ ☐ ☐
Can you name three problems at school?	(p.77)	☐ ☐ ☐

Clothes

Can you name ten items of clothing?	(p.80)	☐ ☐ ☐
Can you say you're looking for a coat?	(p.80)	☐ ☐ ☐
Can you say you're size 38/medium?	(p.80)	☐ ☐ ☐
Can you ask to try something on?	(p.80)	☐ ☐ ☐
Can you say it's too expensive/cheap?	(p.80)	☐ ☐ ☐

Complete the grammar

- Fill in the gaps as you revise to test your understanding.
- You could photocopy these pages if you wanted to do this more than once.
- You'll also end up with a concise set of notes on key grammar.
- Check your answers on page 122.

The and a

Fill in the blanks to complete the French words for 'the' and 'a'.

masculine nouns: | le | = 'the' | | = 'a'

feminine nouns: | | = 'the' | | = 'a'

nouns beginning a, e, i, o, u, h | | = 'the'

plural nouns: | | = 'the'

Avoir and être

Complete the parts of *avoir* (to have) and *être* (to be) and check on page 11 to see if you have got them right.

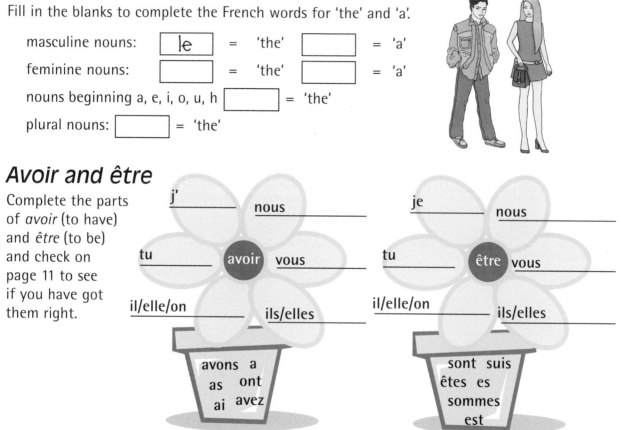

avoir: j' ___ nous ___ tu ___ vous ___ il/elle/on ___ ils/elles ___

avons   a
as   ont
ai   avez

être: je ___ nous ___ tu ___ vous ___ il/elle/on ___ ils/elles ___

sont   suis
êtes   es
sommes
est

Regular verb endings

Complete the verbs and check on page 9 to see if you have got them right.

'er' verb – porter (to wear)		'ir' verb – finir (to finish)		're' verb attendre (to wait)	
je	port e	fini		j'attend	
tu	port	fini		attend	
il/elle/on	port	fini		attend	
nous	port		fini		attend	
vous	port		fini		attend	
ils/elles	port		fini		attend	

Four irregular verbs

Complete these irregular verbs and check on page 31 to see if you have got them right.

	aller (to go)	faire (to do)	vouloir (to want)	pouvoir (to be able to)
je	vais			
tu		fais	veux	
il/elle/on				peut
nous	allons			
vous		faites		pouvez
ils/elles			veulent	

Adjectives

1   Put the adjectives below in the right column.

masculine singular	feminine singular	masculine plural	feminine plural
grand	grande	grands	grandes

blanche   beaux   vieux   beau   vieilles   blanches

nouveau   vieille   belles   nouvelle   vieux

nouveaux   blancs   belle   blanc

nouvelles

2   Can you fill in the forms of *petit, intelligent* and *bleu* now?

My, your, his/her etc.

Complete the grid with the words from below. Check on page 13 to see if you've got it right.

	m. singular	f. singular	plural
my	mon (oncle)	ma (tante)	mes (cousins)
your (*tu*)			
his/her			
our			
your (*vous*)			
their			

tes   vos   leurs
votre   leur   notre
ton   ma   sa   mes
ta   notre   leur
votre   nos
ses   son   mon

Du, de la, des

How would you ask for 'some' of these things? Complete the blanks with *du*, *de la*, *de l'* or *des*.

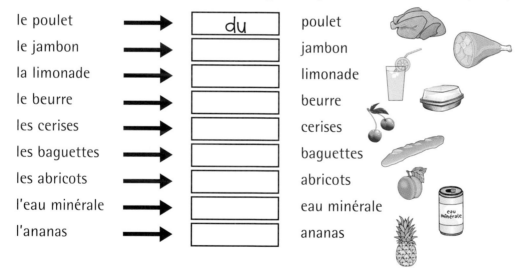

le poulet ➡ [du] poulet

le jambon ➡ [ ] jambon

la limonade ➡ [ ] limonade

le beurre ➡ [ ] beurre

les cerises ➡ [ ] cerises

les baguettes ➡ [ ] baguettes

les abricots ➡ [ ] abricots

l'eau minérale ➡ [ ] eau minérale

l'ananas ➡ [ ] ananas

This and these

How would you say 'this/these' in these sentences? Complete the blanks with *ce*, *cet*, *cette* and *ces*.

le manteau ➡ J'aime [ce] manteau.

le pantalon ➡ J'adore [ ] pantalon rouge.

l'anorak (m) ➡ Je n'aime pas [ ] anorak.

l'imperméable (m) ➡ J'ai acheté [ ] imperméable à Paris.

la robe ➡ [ ] robe est trop petite.

la jupe ➡ [ ] jupe est très jolie.

les baskets ➡ [ ] baskets sont trop chers.

les pantoufles ➡ Je déteste porter [ ] pantoufles.

Reflexive pronouns

Fill in the missing pronoun each time and check on page 21 to see if you've got them right.

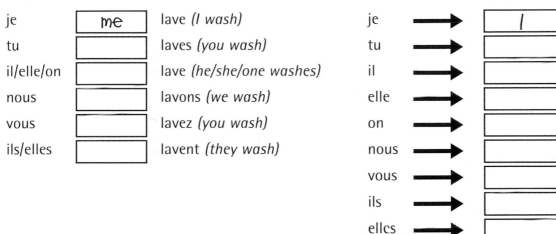

je	**me**	lave *(I wash)*
tu		laves *(you wash)*
il/elle/on		lave *(he/she/one washes)*
nous		lavons *(we wash)*
vous		lavez *(you wash)*
ils/elles		lavent *(they wash)*

Pronouns

What do these pronouns mean in English? Check on page 23 to see if you have got them right.

je	→	*I*
tu	→	
il	→	
elle	→	
on	→	
nous	→	
vous	→	
ils	→	
elles	→	

Four tenses

Complete the flow chart to show the forms of *être* (to be), *avoir* (to have), *faire* (to make) and *aller* (to go) in four tenses. Check on page 96 to see if you have got them right.

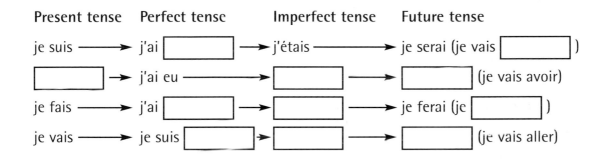

Present tense	Perfect tense	Imperfect tense	Future tense
je suis ⟶	j'ai ☐ ⟶	j'étais ⟶	je serai (je vais ☐)
☐ →	j'ai eu ⟶	☐ →	☐ (je vais avoir)
je fais ⟶	j'ai ☐ →	☐ →	je ferai (je ☐)
je vais ⟶	je suis ☐ ▸	☐ →	☐ (je vais aller)

Future expressions

Complete the French for these expressions, used to talk about the future.

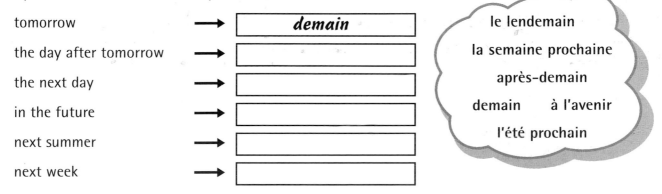

tomorrow	→	***demain***
the day after tomorrow	→	
the next day	→	
in the future	→	
next summer	→	
next week	→	

le lendemain

la semaine prochaine

après-demain

demain   à l'avenir

l'été prochain

The perfect tense

Past participles

1 Complete this chart to show how to form past participles.

er verb: écouter ⟶ écouter ⟶ é = [   ]

ir verb: finir ⟶ finir ⟶ i = [   ]

re verb: descendre ⟶ [   ] ⟶ u = descendu

2 Complete this grid with past participles. Watch out for the irregular ones marked *.

	+ avoir			+ être
avoir* (to have)	j'ai eu	aller (to go)		je suis allé(e)
écouter (to hear)		arriver (to arrive)		
jouer (to play)		entrer (to enter)		
faire* (to do)		partir (to leave)		
manger (to eat)		rester (to stay)		
boire* (to drink)		tomber (to fall)		
écrire* (to write)		monter (to go up)		
lire* (to read)		descendre (to go down)		
prendre* (to take)		venir* (to come)		
voir* (to see)		me laver (to wash)		

3 Complete the French for these expressions, used to talk about the past.

yesterday ⟶ **hier**

the day before yesterday ⟶ [   ]

before ⟶ [   ]

in the past ⟶ [   ]

last Saturday ⟶ [   ]

last year ⟶ [   ]

last summer ⟶ [   ]

dans le passé

samedi dernier   avant

hier   l'été dernier

l'année dernière

avant-hier

Verbs with an infinitive

Make nine sentences from this grid.

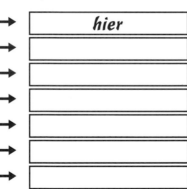

J'adore (I love)		lire		la télé
J'aime (I like)		aider		de la musique
Je déteste (I hate)		aller		du café
Je n'aime pas (I dislike)		jouer		au cinéma
Je voudrais (I'd like to)		écouter		des chips
J'aimerais bien (I'd like to)		faire		des romans
Je vais (I'm going to)		manger		à la maison
J'ai l'intention de (I intend to)		boire		mes devoirs
Il me faut (I have to)		regarder		aux cartes

My world

All about me

B Birthdays (page 8)

Q janvier, février, juillet, septembre, octobre, novembre, décembre

A Personal details (page 10)

2 Je m'appelle John Nugent. N.U.G.E.N.T. (ehn ewe zhay er ehn tay). C'est le seize juin. J'ai quinze ans. Je suis écossais. Oui, j'ai une souris et un cochon d'inde.

B Personal descriptions (page 10)

2 a Je m'appelle Paul et j'ai seize ans. J'ai les yeux bleus et les cheveux courts et bruns. Je suis mince et je porte des lunettes. b Je m'appelle Béatrice et j'ai quatorze ans. J'ai les yeux bleus et les cheveux longs et blonds. Je suis grande et je porte des lunettes. c Je m'appelle Susanne et j'ai quinze ans. J'ai les yeux verts et les cheveux courts et bruns/marron. Je suis petite.

C An ID form (page 11)

2 boy/girl, single/married,
   1 forename and surname,
   2 nationality,
   3 address (with postcode),
   4 telephone number,
   5 age,
   6 birthday,
   7 animals,
   8 hair/eyes,
   9 height/weight

Q *célibataire* means single

Family and friends

Practice (page 13)

oncle, mère, frère, sœur, père, tante, cousin(e)

A Yvonne's family (page 14)

1 *mère* – mother, *beau-père* – step-father, *sœur* – sister, *demi-frère* – half-brother, *parents* – parents

C Positives and negatives (page 15)

2 a P, b N, c N, d P, e P+N, f N, g N, h P+N

Practice (page 15)

responsible, obliging, intelligent, polite, friendly (amicable)

House and home

Practice (page 17)

a la moquette/le tapis, b le lit, c les rideaux, d le jardin, e la maison jumelle, f la cuisine, g le mur, h la douche, i la salle de bains, j le rez-de-chaussée

A Opinions about your home area (page 18)

1 a, b, d, f

Q polluted due to large factories

B My house (page 19)

Q table, computer, two beds, wardrobe, chair, posters, hi-fi, TV; listen to music, play on computer, drink cola, do homework

2 a dans la banlieue de Nice, b une pelouse et des fleurs, c au rez-de-chaussée, d jolie/aux murs orange/à la moquette bleue, e son petit frère, f oui, g écoutent de la musique, jouent à l'ordinateur et boivent du coca, h non

School

A All about school (page 22)

3 1 c, 2 f, 3 d, 4 e, 5 g, 6 a, 7 b

B Clocks (page 22)

2 Il est ... a douze heures et quart, b trois heures moins cinq, c huit heures et demie, d onze heures moins cinq, e huit heures vingt, f dix heures dix, g quatre heures moins le quart, h une heure

C My school (page 23)

Q music, art, technology, sport, science, maths, English, history

2 a 30, b technical college, c (any three) labs, music, art and technology classrooms, library, sports centre d he's good at sport, e 7:10

Holiday time and travel

Visiting a town

B Shops (page 24)

Q closed on Wednesdays

Practice (page 25)

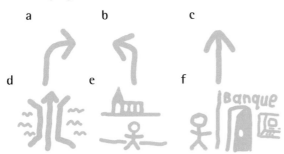

Visiting a town

A Signs (page 26)

1 a crêperie, b baker, c town centre, d medical lab, e town hall, f café, g butcher/deli, h stations

Q the pâtisserie is open on Sundays

Q hungry: a, b, f, g

3 1 h, 2 b, 3 g, 4 c, 5 d, 6 a

B Shopping centre plan (page 27)

2 a, d, f, h

Q oui – on peut acheter un livre

Practice (page 27)

Exemple: Tu vas à gauche et puis tu prends la première rue à droite. Tu continues tout droit. Tu prends la deuxième rue à droite et tu vas jusqu'aux feux. Là tu vas à droite et ma maison se trouve dans cette rue à droite.

Transport

C Extras (page 28)

Q Deux allers simples pour Paris, s'il vous plaît.

Practice (page 29)

1 f, 2 h, 3 c, 4 e, 5 g, 6 i, 7 d, 8 b, 9 a

A Key train phrases (page 30)

1 a un aller simple, b un aller retour pour Rouen, c Le train part à quelle heure? d non-fumeur, e un billet de première classe, f Le train arrive à quelle heure? g Le train part de quel quai?

B Role play – at the train station (page 30)

3 1 Bonjour. 2 Un aller retour pour Bordeaux, s'il vous plaît. 3 Deuxième classe, s'il vous plaît. 4 Ça coûte combien? 5 A quelle heure part le train? 6 Merci beaucoup. Au revoir.

Q Bonjour. Au revoir.

C Transport (page 31)

2 Dix personnes vont à pied. Huit personnes vont en autobus. Sept personnes vont en métro. Cinq personnes vont par le train. Trois personnes vont en voiture. Deux personnes vont en vélo. Une personne va en avion.

Practice (page 31)

a Il est douze heures vingt-quatre. b Il est dix-sept heures trente. c Il est onze heures seize. d Il est vingt-trois heures quarante-cinq. e Il est dix-neuf heures trente-cinq. f Il est sept heures cinq. g Il est vingt heures cinquante et un.

Holiday time

Practice (page 33)

Je suis allé(e)... a en Angleterre, b en Suisse, c en Belgique, d en Autriche, e au Canada, f en France, g en Espagne, h au Portugal, i en Russie

A European destinations (page 34)

Q Londres

2 1 E, 2 B, 3 F, 4 H, 5 A, 6 D, 7 G, 8 C

B Holiday adverts (page 35)

Q February: holiday 1

Q breakfast

3 a 2, b 2, c 1, d 2, e 3, f 1, g 1, h 3

Accommodation

Practice (page 37)

Est-ce que je peux louer ... a des draps? b un vélo tout-terrain (VTT)? c un bateau? d un sac de couchage?

A Campsite adverts (page 38)

2 a 1, b 2, c 2, d 1, e 1, f 2

Q 1 splendid views, 2 views of the beach

B Visiting a penfriend (page 39)

Q Emilie left: soap, toothpaste, pyjamas, slippers

3 e, b, d, a, f, c, g

Hotel and weather

A Booking into a hotel (page 40)

Q une chambre pour deux personnes

A Hotel questions (page 42)

1 a (Je voudrais) une chambre pour deux personnes avec douche, s'il vous plaît. b Pour quatre nuits. c Ça coûte combien? d Est-ce qu'il y a une piscine dans l'hôtel? e C'est quand, le petit déjeuner?

B Hotel booking letter (page 42)

1 a Cannes le 4 mai, b Hôtel du Pont, 34, rue Ravel, 79308 Niort, c Monsieur, d Je vous prie d'agréer, Monsieur, l'expression de mes sentiments distingués.

2 a 5–8 April, b for a conference, c single room, d by car, e parking space

C The weather (page 43)

2 a Bordeaux, b les Alpes, c Calais, d Nice, e Strasbourg, f Paris

Practice (page 43)

map: vendredi

Public services

C Post (page 44)

Q Six timbres à cinquante cents, s'il vous plaît.

D Reporting a loss (page 45)

Q J'ai perdu mon sac bleu. Il y avait un livre rouge et des clés dedans.

Practice (page 45)

a Bonjour, b une carte postale, c cents, d une lettre, e timbres, f tout, g paquet, h euros, i Au revoir

Public services

A Using a phone box (page 46)

2 1 f, 2 i, 3 h, 4 d, 5 e, 6 c, 7 a, 8 g, 9 b

Q entre, décroche, introduis, attend, compose, parle, raccroche, retire, quitte

B Lost and found (page 47)

3 a 2, b 6, c 4, d 1, e 5, f 3

Q two pens, pencils, ruler, rubber

Practice (page 47)

a Yves Mulot, b dans la bibliothèque, c mercredi, le 12 février, d gris et jaune, e trousse

Work and lifestyle

Free time

Practice (page 49)

a basket, b vélo, c ski, d football, e tennis de table, f natation, g voile, h tennis

A Hobbies (page 50)

2 1 b, 2 d, 3 e, 4 c, 5 a

Q hobby d (*danser*)

C Sports (page 51)

2 *sportif*: a, c, d, g, h; *non*: b, e, f

Q (any six) skiing, ice hockey, roller skating, baseball, football, rugby, climbing, running, tennis, swimming

Media

A TV and music questionaire (page 54)

Q Mon groupe préféré, c'est...

B At the cinema (page 55)

Q 18 euros 40, 2 hours 20 minutes

Practice (page 55)

- Trois places pour salle deux, s'il vous plaît.
- Il y a des réductions pour les enfants?
- Alors, ça fait vingt-quatre euros.
- Il commence à dix-sept heures vingt. Il finit à dix-neuf heures quarante-cinq.
- C'est en français.

Jobs

B Places of work (page 56)

Q Je travaille dans une école/un hôpital.

Practice (page 57)

a professeur, b fermier, c pilote, d boulangère, e médecin, f facteur, g serveuse

Q b *fermier* is male as *fermière* is female form, d *boulangère* is female as *boulanger* is male form, f *facteur* is male as *factrice* is female form, g *serveuse* is female as *serveur* is male form

A Job descriptions (page 58)

2 a On est professeur. b On est infirmier/infirmière ou médecin. c On est mécanicien(ne). d On est steward/hôtesse de l'air.

B Family jobs (page 58)

1 a, c, e, g

Q he retired

B A CV (page 59)

2 1 Alain Dupont, 2 dix-huit ans, 3 3 décembre 1989, 4 Toulouse, 5 français, 6 Herbert Dupont (journaliste), 7 Karine Dupont (vendeuse), 8 10, rue de Breil, 35051 Rennes, 9 60.98.67.97, 10 1994–2001: l'école primaire à Toulouse; de 2001: Lycée St.-Germain, Rennes, 11 ordinateurs/le cinéma, 12 distribue les journaux, 13 programmeur

Teenage work

Practice (page 61)

Jean fait du babysitting. Henri travaille dans un supermarché. Patrice distribue les journaux. Anna fait du jardinage. Olivier travaille comme serveur/dans un café. Jacques fait le repassage. Julie nettoie les fenêtres.

A Helping at home (page 62)

3 1 j, 2 e, 3 i, 4 c, 5 a, 6 f, 7 d, 8 b, 9 g, 10 h

Q brother

B Job adverts (page 63)

Q in the mornings

2 Virginie 1, Julie 3, Matthieu 2

Q positions 1 and 2

Practice (page 63)

a yes, b no, c yes, d two girls aged two and six, e July–October, f seven hours from 06:00–13:00

Health

D Higher numbers (page 65)

Q 68 soixante-huit, 99 quatre-vingt-dix-neuf, 112 cent douze, 2456 deux mille quatre cents cinquante-six

A Illnesses (page 66)

2 1 c, 2 a, 3 b, 4 c, 5 b, 6 a, 7 c

Q J'ai un rhume et de la fièvre et le dos me fait mal.

B Buying fruit and vegetables (page 67)

1 Trois cents grammes de haricots verts, un demi kilo de carottes, un kilo de pommes de terre, une douzaine de poires, une boîte de tomates, des framboises et deux choux-fleurs, s'il vous plaît.

Practice (page 67)

a 5, b 7, c 8, d 6, e 1, f 9, g 3, h 2, i 4

Food and drink

B Drinks (page 68)

Q Une tasse de thé avec du sucre et du lait, s'il vous plaît.

Practice (page 69)

1 b, 2 c, 3 a, 4 a, 5 c, 6 a, 7 c

A Food and drink items (page 70)

1

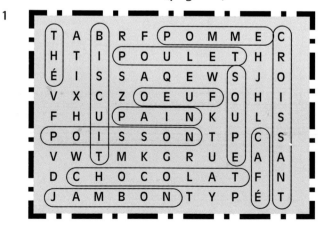

C Cafés (page 71)

2 Jean 3, Tim 1, Katherine 2

Q Jean would like hamburger, sausage and chicken

Q 'matin' = morning and 'petit déjeuner' = breakfast

Practice (page 71)

Paul mange du poulet et de la glace. Emilie mange du fromage et du pain et elle boit de la limonade. Frank mange du saucisson, du riz et du yaourt. Yves mange des pâtes, du potage et du chocolat.

Young person in society

Teenage concerns

Practice (page 73)

tabac: a, g; alcool: b, d, e; drogues: c, f, h

Q dancing, meeting young people and drinking

B Phrases for discussing issues (page 74)

1 1 f, 2 a, 3 g, 4 b, 5 d, 6 c, 7 e, 8 h

C An environmental action ⓗ (page 75)

a elle s'inscrit à un groupe qui travaille sur l'environnement, b au recyclage, c de la cantine, d il les emporte dans la cour de l'école quand elles sont pleines, e tous les jours, f elle aide à nettoyer la cour de l'école

Practice (page 75)

a 3, b 6, c 4, d 1, e 5, f 2

Adolescent life

A Adolescent life (page 78)

3 a Jean-Philippe, Vincent, Yasmine, b Yasmine, c Vincent, d Vincent, e Isabelle, f Isabelle, g Jean-Philippe

Q père (father), belle-mère (step-mother), parents, mère (mother), enfants (children), beau-père (step-father)

Practice (page 79)

(any three) no smoking, no drug-taking, no being rude to teachers, have to do homework; violence, graffiti, vandalism

Fashion

C Describing clothes (page 81)

1 jupe, chaussures, blouson, robe, chemise, pantalon

D At a clothes shop (page 81)

2 f, d, h, c, g, b, e, a

Q size thirty

Listening

A Favourite school subjects (page 82)

4 la biologie (*twice*), l'anglais, les sciences naturelles, la musique, le français, les mathématiques, le sport, les sciences physiques

B Least favourite subjects (page 82)

2 l'anglais (*twice*), les mathématiques (*twice*)

C Julien's room (page 83)

3 le salon 1, 3, 7, 8, 10; la chambre de Julien 2, 5, 6, 11

Q 2 un lit = a bed

D Julien's daily routine (page 83)

3 a se réveille, b sept heures dix, c salle de bains, d trente, e petit-déjeuner, f tartines, g chocolat chaud, h huit, i quitte

E Brothers and sisters (page 84)

2 Listen and note the answers.

3 1 d, 2 c, 3 c, 4 c, 5 d, 6 a, 7 d, 8 a/c, 9 e

F Ages (page 84)

2 1 5, 2 3/7, 3 16/3, 4 16, 5 8.5, 6 10, 7 15, 8 23

G Clémentine's family (page 85)

2 <u>travaille</u> = works, <u>habite</u> = lives, <u>aime</u> = likes

4 Mère - nom: Chantal, Age: 43, Travail: à la bibliothèque, Adore: les mots-croisés, Caractère: un peu snob. Frère - nom: Emile, Age: 11, Caractère: mignon, Adore: le foot, Aime le plus: les rats, A combien: 40. Père - Travail: à la poste, Passe-temps: jouer aux boules, aller au café, Caractère: très gentil

5 1 à la bibliothèque, 2 43, 3 une tasse du thé, 4 le petit frère de Clémentine, 5 les photos de ses joueurs préfrés, 6 ses rats, 7 le père de Clémentine, 8 6:30, 9 ses amis, 10 oui, elle adore son père

H Sports (page 86)

3 1 e, 2 d, 3 b/c/f, 4 c, 5 c, 6 a/f/h, 7 f/g

I Dijon (page 86)

2 1, 4, 5, 6, 8

J Jobs (page 87)

3 1 professeur, 2 médecin, 3 conducteur de train, 4 au chômage, 5 banquier

K Working hours (page 87)

2 1 08:00 2 08:00 3 08:30 4 07:00 5 16:40 6 19:00 7 22:00

L Adverts (page 88)

Q manger (*to eat*), boire (*to drink*), porter (*to wear/carry*), voir (*to see*), sentir (*to smell*), jouer (*to play*)

3 1 a, 2 c, 3 c, 4 b, 5 b

M Countries (page 89)

3 1 France, 2 France, 3 France, 4 Germany, 5 Belgium, 6 England, 7 Italy, 8 Canada, 9 Switzerland

N Hotel Canelle (page 89)

2 1 13 ans, 2 directeur de l'hôtel, 3 150, 4 au bord de la plage, 5 (*any three*) fruit, pain, yaourts, fromage, jambon 6 (*any four*) la piscine, la mer, les boules, le club de voile, la plage, le club pour les enfants, le restaurant, le bateau, les îles

Q <u>petit déjeuner</u> = breakfast

Complete the grammar

The and a (page 108)

le/un, la/une, l', les

Adjectives (page 109)

grand, grande, grands, grandes; blanc, blanche, blancs, blanches; beau, belle, beaux, belles; vieux, vieille, vieux, vieilles; nouveau, nouvelle, nouveaux, nouvelles; petit, petite, petits, petites; intelligent, intelligente, intelligents, intelligentes; bleu, bleue, bleus, bleues.

Du, de la, des (page 110)

du poulet, du jambon, de la limonade, de beurre, des cerises, des baguettes, des abricots, de l'eau minérale, de l'ananas

This and these (page 110)

ce manteau, ce pantalon rouge, cet anarok, cet imperméable, Cette robe, Cette jupe, Ces baskets, ces pantoufles

Future expressions (page 111)

demain, après-demain, le lendemain, à l'avenir, l'été prochain, la semaine prochaine

The perfect tense (page 112)

1 écouté, fini, descendre

2 j'ai eu, j'ai écouté, j'ai joué, j'ai fait, j'ai mangé, j'ai bu, j'ai écrit, j'ai lu, j'ai pris, j'ai vu

   je suis allé(e), je suis arrivé(e), je suis entré(e), je suis parti(e), je suis resté(e), je suis tombé(e), je suis monté(e), je suis descendu(e), je suis venu(e), je me suis lavé(e)

3 hier, avant-hier, avant, dans la passé, samedi dernier, l'année dernière, l'été dernier

Last-minute learner

- The next six pages give you the key vocabulary across the whole subject in the smallest possible space.
- You can use these pages as a final check.
- You can also use them as you revise as a way to check your learning.
- You can cut them out for quick and easy reference.

Letters and numbers

Alphabet (p.9)

a ah, **b** bay, **c** say, **d** day, **e** er, **f** ehf, **g** zhay, **h** ahsh, **i** ee, **j** zhee, **k** kah, **l** ehl, **m** ehm, **n** ehn, **o** oh, **p** pay, **q** kew, **r** ehr, **s** ehss, **t** tay, **u** ewe, **v** vay, **w** doobler vay, **x** eeks **y** ee grehk, **z** zehd

Numbers (p.8)

zéro	0	quinze	15	soixante-treize	73	quatre vingt-douze	92
un	1	seize	16	soixante-quatorze	74	quatre-vingt-treize	93
deux	2	dix-sept	17	soixante-quinze	75	quatre-vingt-quatorze	94
trois	3	dix-huit	18	soixante-seize	76	quatre-vingt-quinze	95
quatre	4	dix-neuf	19	soixante-dix-sept	77	quatre-vingt-seize	96
cinq	5	vingt	20	soixante-dix-huit	78	quatre-vingt-dix-sept	97
six	6	vingt et un	21	soixante-dix-neuf	79	quatre-vingt-dix-huit	98
sept	7	vingt-deux	22	quatre-vingts	80	cent	100
huit	8	trente	30	quatre-vingt-un	81	cent un	101
neuf	9	quarante	40	quatre-vingt-deux	82	deux cents	200
dix	10	cinquante	50	quatre-vingt-trois	83	mille	1000
onze	11	soixante	60	quatre-vingt-quatre	84	deux mille	2000
douze	12	soixante-dix	70	quatre-vingt-dix	90	deux mille dix	2010
treize	13	soixante et onze	71	quatre-vingt-onze	91		
quatorze	14	soixante-douze	72				

Calendar (p.8)

Days
lundi, mardi, mercredi, jeudi, vendredi, samedi, dimanche

Months
janvier, février, mars, avril, mai, juin, juillet, août, septembre, octobre, novembre, décembre

Seasons
le printemps/au printemps   l'été/en été
l'automne/en automne   l'hiver/en hiver

Greetings and being polite (p.13)

Salut/Bonjour/Au revoir, Bonsoir/Bonne nuit, Bon voyage! Bienvenue. Bon week-end. Joyeux Noël! Joyeuses Pâques! Bonne fête! Bon anniversaire! Ça va? Ça va bien, merci. Ça ne va pas. S'il vous plaît/Merci. Je te/vous remercie beaucoup. De rien.

Writing letters

Informal letter
- *place and date on right-hand side*: Nantes, le 15 février
- *to a boy* = Cher (Michael/Oliver)
- *to a girl* = Chère (Anna/Rebecca)
- *endings:* grosses bises, amicalement, à bientôt
- *ton* (from a boy)/*ta* (from a girl)

Formal letter
- *place and date on right-hand side*: Nantes, le 15 février
- *to a man* = Cher Monsieur X
- *to a woman* = Chère Madame Y
- *to strangers* = Monsieur/Madame
- *ending*: Je vous prie d'agréer, Madame/Monsieur, l'expression de mes sentiments distingués

Time (p.21 and p.28)

The 12-hour clock
Quelle heure est-il?
Il est une heure. Il est deux/quatre heures. Il est une heure cinq/dix. Il est deux heures et quart. Il est deux heures et demie. Il est trois heures moins le quart. Il est trois heures moins dix/cinq. Il est minuit/midi.

The 24-hour clock
Il est une heure dix. Il est dix heures quinze. Il est treize heures quarante. Il est seize heures vingt. Il est dix-huit heures. Il est vingt-deux heures trente.

Colours (p.9 and p.45)

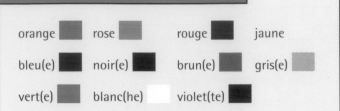

orange   rose   rouge   jaune

bleu(e)   noir(e)   brun(e)   gris(e)

vert(e)   blanc(he)   violet(te)

Countries (p.32)

l'Allemagne, les Etats-Unis, l'Angleterre, la Belgique, le Canada, l'Ecosse, l'Espagne, la France, la Grande-Bretagne, la Grèce, la Hollande, l'Irlande, l'Italie, le Pays de Galles, le Portugal, la Suisse

Section 1: My world (p.8)

All about me
Je m'appelle (Darren Highcliff). J'ai (quinze/seize) ans.
Mon anniversaire est le (sept février).
Je suis (anglais(e)/écossais(e)/irlandais(e)/gallois(e)).
J'ai les yeux (bleus/verts/bruns).
J'ai les cheveux (bruns/marron/blonds/noirs) et (raides/frisés/longs/courts).
Je suis (petit(e)/mince/grand(e)/gros(se)).
J'ai (un chien/un chat/un poisson rouge/une tortue).

Family
J'ai (un frère/une sœur). Je suis fils/fille unique. (Mon frère) est plus âgé/jeune que moi. Je suis l'aîné(e). J'habite avec (mes parents/ma mère/mon beau-père). Mes parents sont divorcés/séparés. Je m'entends bien avec (ma belle-mère/mon grand-père/ma tante).

Friends

Mon copain/Ma copine est (marrant(e), intelligent(e), travailleur (travailleuse), patient(e), poli(e), content(e)).

Mon ami(e) est (impatient(e), égoïste, méchant(e), bête, paresseux (paresseuse), timide).

Rooms and furniture
la cuisine, la salle à manger, la chambre, la salle de bains, le salon/la salle de séjour, le bureau, les WC, la cave
Dans ma chambre, il y a (un fauteuil, une armoire, un placard, une chaise, un lit, une table, des posters, un ordinateur). Mes vêtements sont dans l'armoire. Il y a des disquettes sur/sous la table. Dans la cuisine, il y a (un four, une machine à laver, un lave-vaisselle, un frigo). Dans la salle de bains, il y a (une douche, des toilettes, une baignoire, un lavabo, un miroir).

My house
J'habite (un appartement de (six) pièces, une maison jumelle/individuelle). Nous avons un grand/petit jardin. La cuisine se trouve au rez-de-chaussée. Il y a trois pièces au premier étage. J'ai ma propre chambre. J'habite dans (le sud/nord/l'ouest/l'est/une ville/un village/une ferme/la banlieue). J'habite (à la campagne/au bord de la mer/sur la côte/au centre-ville). Notre bâtiment est (vieux/moderne/laid/beau/grand/petit). Ma ville/La région est (historique/industrielle/touristique/belle). Il y a (mille) habitants dans mon village.

School subjects
Ma matière préférée, c'est (le français/la biologie/la musique). J'aime bien (l'allemand/l'informatique/l'histoire/les sciences). Je n'aime pas (l'espagnol/la géographie/l'art dramatique). Je déteste (la physique/la religion/la technologie). Je suis fort(e) en (allemand/éducation physique). Je suis nul(le) en (maths/chimie). J'aime (le sport) parce que c'est intéressant/facile. Je n'aime pas (le dessin) parce que c'est difficile/nul.

In school
Je vais à un (C.E.S./lycée technique/lycée mixte/collège privé). Il y a (un centre sportif/une bibliothèque/23 salles de classe, un laboratoire, une cantine, une cour). Je suis en (quatrième/troisième). Il y a environ (mille) élèves dans mon collège. Mon lycée est (vieux/grand/moderne). Je porte un uniforme (gris et noir).

Daily routine
Je me réveille. Je me lève. Je me lave. Je m'habille. Je prends le petit déjeuner. Je quitte la maison. Le premier cours commence. La récréation est à (dix heures). Le déjeuner est à (midi). Les cours finissent à (deux heures). Je fais mes devoirs. Le soir je mange à (huit heures). Je prends un bain. Je me couche.

Places in town
Dans ma ville, il y a un (marché, aéroport, stade, musée, château, cinéma, théâtre, hôtel de ville, office de tourisme). Il n'y a pas de (cathédrale, église, mairie, piscine, gare, université, bibliothèque).

Shops
ouvert/fermé, une librairie, une boutique, une boucherie, une parfumerie, une boulangerie, une pâtisserie, une charcuterie, un bureau de tabac, une confiserie, une épicerie, une pharmacie, un supermarché, un grand magasin, un hypermarché, un marché, un centre commercial

Finding the way
Excusez-moi. Pardon? Où sont (les toilettes/téléphones), s'il vous plaît? Où se trouve (l'arrêt d'autobus? C'est ici à gauche/droite. Allez tout droit. Prenez la première/deuxième rue à droite/gauche. Traversez le pont/la place. Allez jusqu'au carrefour. Tournez à droite/gauche (au rond-point/aux feux). C'est au coin de/en face de/entre/à côté de/près de/derrière/devant (la gare).

Buying a train ticket
Un aller simple/retour pour (Calais), s'il vous plaît. Première ou deuxième classe? Fumeur ou non-fumeur? Le train est direct? Il faut changer à (Lyon). Le train part de quel quai? Le train part/arrive à quelle heure? Est-ce qu'il faut faire une réservation?

Forms of transport
Je vais à pied. Je vais en (bus/car/voiture/taxi/avion/camion). J'aime aller en (train/métro).

A past holiday
Je suis allé(e) à (Nice/Paris). J'ai voyagé en (voiture/train/car/avion/bateau/bus). Je suis resté(e) à la maison. J'ai passé (un mois/quinze jours/une semaine) en France. L'année dernière, je suis allé(e) à l'étranger. J'étais (sur la côte/à la montagne/au bord de la mer). Je suis resté(e) (dans un camping/une auberge de jeunesse/un hôtel/chez mes cousins). Il faisait beau/mauvais. J'ai (nagé dans la piscine/visité la cathédrale/acheté des souvenirs).

Youth hostel
Une auberge de jeunesse, le lit, le dortoir. Est-ce que je peux louer (un VTT/un bateau/du linge/des draps/une serviette)? Il est interdit de manger dans les dortoirs. Défense de fumer dans l'auberge. Vous êtes priés de quitter le bâtiment à dix heures. On ferme la porte d'entrée à vingt-trois heures.

Campsite
Le camping a (une piscine/un supermarché/une laverie). J'aime/Je déteste faire du camping. On a besoin d'(une tente/une caravane/une allumette/un sac de couchage/un ouvre-boîte/un canif).

Staying with a penfriend
Je veux te/vous présenter ma famille. Enchanté(e), Madame/Monsieur. Je n'ai pas de (dentifrice/savon/brosse à dents. Merci pour votre hospitalité. Le séjour était bon/affreux. C'était une visite agréable.

Hotel
Avez-vous une chambre libre? Je voudrais une chambre pour (une personne/deux personnes). Pour deux (enfants/adultes/nuits). Ça coûte 128 euros par personne par nuit. Avec salle de bains/douche? Il y a (un ascenseur/un parking/une piscine/de la climatisation) à l'hôtel? Pension complète. Demi-pension. Chiens (non) admis. C'est à quelle heure, le dîner? Est-ce qu'il y a (une télévision/des toilettes/un balcon) dans la chambre?

The weather
Quel temps fait-il? Il fait (beau/chaud/froid). Il fait (du brouillard/soleil/vent). Il y a des averses. Il gèle/neige. Il faisait beau/mauvais. Il y avait des nuages.

Telephone
Quel est votre numéro de téléphone? C'est le zéro, dix, vingt, douze, quarante-cinq. C'est X à l'appareil. Allô, Christophe? Est-ce que je peux parler à X? Je suis désolé(e), mais X n'est pas là. Je peux laisser un message? Je rappellerai plus tard. C'est quoi, l'indicatif?

Bank
Où se trouve (la banque/le bureau de change)? Je voudrais changer un chèque de voyage. Il me faut changer des livres sterling en euros. La livre est à combien? Elle est à 1 euro 56. Il faut payer une commission.

Post
Où se trouve (la poste/la boîte aux lettres)? Je voudrais envoyer (une lettre/une carte postale/un paquet) en France. Je voudrais trois timbres à deux euros. Quatre timbres pour l'Angleterre, s'il vous plaît. C'est combien?

Reporting a loss
Où se trouve le bureau des objets trouvés? J'ai perdu mon (téléphone portable/sac à main/sac à dos/mon passeport/mon appareil-photo/portefeuille/porte-monnaie). J'ai laissé ma (valise/carte de crédit) au café/dans le train. Ça s'est passé ce matin à dix heures trente. Il y avait (des clés/de la monnaie/120 euros) là-dedans.

Reporting an accident
J'étais sur la Route Nationale, la N7/l'autoroute A6. Je conduisais rapidement/trop vite. Je n'ai pas vu le feu rouge. (Police-secours/Une ambulance) est arrivée à toute vitesse. Il ne portait pas de ceinture de sécurité. Je suis allé(e) à l'hôpital. Je n'étais pas blessé(e). Au secours!

Hobbies

J'aime/J'adore (jouer aux cartes/nager/faire du sport/faire du théâtre/écouter de la musique/regarder la télé/jouer du violon/jouer du piano/jouer aux jeux électroniques/aller au cinéma/aller au concert/faire des promenades/retrouver les ami(e)s/aller à la maison des jeunes).
Je déteste/Je n'aime pas (lire).

Sports

Je fais (du vélo/du cyclisme/du cheval/de l'équitation/de la natation/de la planche à voile/de la gymnastique).
Je joue au (football/tennis/basket/volley).
Je vais à la pêche. J'aime courir. Mon sport préféré, c'est (jouer au foot).

How often

Je fais ça (le lundi/le samedi/le soir/tous les jours/souvent/chaque week-end/de temps en temps/l'hiver). Je m'entraîne (chaque week-end).

Television

J'aime bien les (jeux télévisés/films/documentaires/informations/actualités).
Je n'aime pas les (feuilletons/ dessins animés/émissions de sport/émissions de musique).
Je regarde la télévision (tous les jours/chaque soir/une heure par jour). Mon émission préférée, c'est «Les Simpson».

Music

Mon chanteur préféré, c'est X. Ma chanteuse préférée, c'est X. Ma chanson préférée, c'est X. Mon groupe préféré, c'est X. J'adore écouter la musique (pop/rock/classique). J'aime écouter la radio. J'achète des (CDs/cassettes).

Cinema

J'adore les films (comiques/d'épouvante/d'aventure/d'horreur/de science-fiction).
Deux places pour salle trois, s'il vous plaît. Ça fait combien? Il y a des réductions pour les (étudiants/enfants)? Le film commence à quelle heure? La séance finit à quelle heure? C'est en version française/originale? C'est sous-titré.

Theatre

J'adore aller au théâtre. Les acteurs étaient excellents. L'actrice principale était nulle. La musique était formidable. C'était une bonne soirée. Je n'avais pas une bonne place au balcon. C'était une pièce (intéressante/ennuyeuse).

Books

L'histoire n'était pas bonne. Il s'agissait (d'une famille/de la guerre/des copains). Ça se passait en (Italie/France/Allemagne). C'était (triste/amusant/comique/drôle/compliqué/difficile). J'ai beaucoup pleuré/ri. Je l'ai trouvé compliqué. J'aime lire (le journal/les romans/les livres de science-fiction/les bandes dessinées).

Inviting somebody out

Tu es libre ce week-end? Si on allait au cirque? On va au (spectacle/match de foot)? Tu veux (faire une excursion/aller à la discothèque)?
J'accepte ton invitation. Oui, d'accord. Je veux bien.
Ça ne me dit rien. Je regrette/Je suis désolé(e) mais je ne suis pas libre.
On se retrouve (où/à quelle heure)? On se retrouve (à six heures/chez moi/à la gare/à l'école).

Jobs

le boucher	la bouchère
le boulanger	la boulangère
le caissier	la caissière
le coiffeur	la coiffeuse
le directeur	la directrice
un épicier	une épicière
le facteur	la factrice
le fermier	la fermière
un infirmier	une infirmière
le vendeur	la vendeuse
le serveur	la serveuse

un(e) employé(e) de banque/bureau,
le/la mécanicien(ne),
une hôtesse de l'air
Mon père/Ma mère est (chauffeur de taxi, professeur, gendarme, dentiste, médecin, agent de police, ingénieur).
Ma tante est (sans travail/au chômage).

Helping at home

Je fais (la vaisselle/la cuisine/les courses/le jardinage). Je (mets/débarrasse) la table. Je nettoie (la maison/les fenêtres). Je range ma chambre. Je lave mes vêtements. Je sors la poubelle. Je passe l'aspirateur. Je prépare (le petit déjeuner/le déjeuner/le dîner/les repas). Je fais ça (le week-end/toujours/tous les jours/de temps en temps). Je ne passe jamais l'aspirateur. J'aime aider à la maison. Je n'aime pas faire le ménage.

Work experience

J'ai fait un stage d'entreprise. J'ai aidé les clients. J'ai travaillé dans (un bureau/une usine). J'ai (organisé des rendez-vous/tapé et livré des lettres/répondu au téléphone/fait des photocopies/travaillé sur l'ordinateur). Tout le monde était sympa. Les gens étaient horribles.

Part-time work and pocket money

Je fais du (jardinage/babysitting). Je distribue les journaux. Je travaille dans un (café/bureau/supermarché/magasin). Je (commence/finis) à huit heures. Je travaille (le samedi/le week-end/six heures) au magasin. Je gagne six euros de l'heure. Je fais des économies. Je n'ai pas de petit emploi. C'est (varié/intéressant/fatigant/bien payé/mal payé). Mes parents me donnent huit euros par semaine. Je reçois trente euros par mois. Je ne reçois pas d'argent de poche.

Illness

Je me sens malade./Je suis (enrhumé(e)/malade/ fatigué(e)). J'ai mal au (cœur/ventre). J'ai mal à la (gorge/tête). J'ai mal aux dents. Mon (bras/pied/doigt) me fait mal. Mes (pieds/mains/jambes) me font mal. Je me suis coupé le doigt. Je me suis cassé la jambe. J'ai (la grippe/un rhume/de la fièvre). Va (chez le docteur/chez le pharmacien/à l'hôpital). Prends/Prenez (quatre comprimés/ce médicament/du sirop/des pastilles pour la gorge).

Body parts

la tête

une oreille

la bouche

le nez

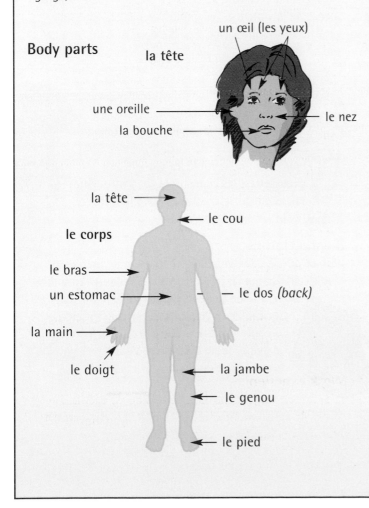

la tête

le cou

le corps

le bras

un estomac

le dos *(back)*

la main

le doigt

la jambe

le genou

le pied

Fruit and vegetables

les fruits: un abricot, un ananas, un citron, une banane, une cerise, une fraise, une framboise, une orange, une pêche, une pomme, une poire, du raisin, une tomate

les légumes: un chou, un chou-fleur, une carotte, une salade, des champignons, des haricots verts, des petits pois, des pommes de terre

Quantities

une boîte de, une douzaine de, cinq cents grammes de, un kilo de, un peu de, beaucoup de/plein de, quelques, des, plusieurs, un paquet de, un pot de, une tranche de, un morceau de, un litre de, une bouteille de

Food

Je n'aime pas/Je déteste (le bœuf, le jambon, le poulet, le porc, le veau, la saucisse, le saucisson, le pâté, le steak, le bifteck). J'aime/J'adore (les fruits de mer, un œuf/les œufs, le pain, les pâtes, le riz, le yaourt, la glace, les chips, le gâteau, la confiture). Je ne mange jamais de (fromage/viande/poisson).

Drinks

la bière, le cidre, le vin rouge/blanc le coca, la limonade, une eau minérale, un Orangina, un café avec lait/sucre, un chocolat chaud, un thé, une tasse de (chocolat), un litre de lait

At a restaurant

Avez-vous une table pour deux personnes? Je voudrais réserver une table pour dix personnes. Pour samedi soir, à huit heures. Désolé, c'est complet. Monsieur!/Mademoiselle! Avez-vous une carte? Qu'est-ce que vous prenez? Un croque-monsieur, s'il vous plaît. Pour commencer, je prendrai les fruits de mer. Je voudrais du vin rouge/blanc. Je vais prendre un coca. Bon appétit! L'addition, s'il vous plaît. Le service (n')est (pas) compris.

Restaurant complaints

Je n'ai pas de (couteau/cuillère/fourchette). Cette tasse est très (sale/vieille). Il y a de la confiture sur l'assiette. La soupe est froide. Le poisson sent mauvais. Ce poulet a un goût désagréable. Cette crêpe est trop sucrée. Il y a trop de (poivre/sel/moutarde/vinaigre/huile). J'ai dû attendre une heure pour ma pizza. Il y a une erreur dans l'addition.

The environment

Il y a trop de
(circulation/camions) sur
les routes. Les
embouteillages sont
(partout/terribles). L'heure
d'affluence est un grand problème.
La qualité de l'air est atroce. La ville est très polluée.
Il y a des déchets partout. Les trottoirs sont sales.
A mon avis on utilise trop d'énergie. Les animaux sont en
danger. Les plantes ont besoin de protection. La pollution
est un problème mondial.
Je porte (des bouteilles au centre de recyclage). Je prends
(les transports en commun). Je vais partout à vélo. Je me
douche tous les matins. Je réduis la température du
chauffage central. Je ferme les (portes/fenêtres). Je
protège les (plantes/animaux) en danger. La pollution de
la mer m'inquiète.

Smoking, alcohol and drugs

Je fume./Je ne fume pas. Je fume dix
cigarettes par jour. Je n'ai pas peur du
cancer. Je me suis habitué(e) à fumer.
Je ne bois pas d'alcool. Je bois du
(vin/cidre). Je bois de la bière chaque jour.
J'ai envie d'arrêter de boire. Je ne prends
pas de drogue. Il me faut perdre l'habitude.
C'est une maladie. Je fais ça (tous les jours/le week-
end/pas souvent). Tous mes ami(e)s font ça le week-end.
Mes ami(e)s m'encouragent. Je trouve ça dangereux.

Future plans

Cette année je vais passer (le bac/les examens). L'année
prochaine je vais (passer en première/quitter l'école/faire
un apprentissage/faire des études à l'étranger/chercher
un emploi sans responsabilité/chercher un travail bien
payé). Si j'ai de bonnes notes, j'irai à
l'université/en fac. Si mes résultats sont
mauvais, je redoublerai. J'aimerais bien
travailler (dans le commerce/dans le
tourisme/à l'étranger/en France). Je
voudrais bien avoir des enfants.

Adolescence

La vie de l'adolescent est pleine de
soucis. J'ai de gros problèmes à
(l'école/la maison). On me brutalise.
Les examens m'inquiètent. Je n'aime
pas mon corps. Je n'ai pas de
(petit(e) ami(e)/copains/argent).
Je veux quitter l'école. J'ai peur
de la violence. Je me sens tout(e) seul(e). Je ne peux
pas communiquer avec les autres. Je n'ai jamais la
permission (de sortir le samedi soir/d'aller aux
fêtes). Je m'entends bien avec ma mère. Je me
dispute beaucoup avec mon père. Ma
mère n'aime pas mes piercings. Mes
parents (me critiquent/sont trop
sévères). Il y a (peu/beaucoup) de
disputes chez nous.

Problems at school

Au collège on a trop de règles. On ne doit
pas (porter de bijoux/se maquiller/fumer). Il
y a une bonne/mauvaise discipline. Les profs
sont trop sévères. Je suis toujours en retenue. Les élèves
attaquent souvent les autres élèves. J'ai peur de la
violence dans la salle de classe. L'enseignement souffre à
cause de la violence. Les grands problèmes sont les
graffiti et le vandalisme. Peu d'élèves causent beaucoup
de problèmes.

Clothes

le manteau, l'imperméable, l'anorak,
la veste, la chemise, la cravate, le
jean, le short, le jogging, le pantalon,
le pyjama, le sweat-shirt, le T-shirt, le
pull, la jupe, la robe, les baskets, les
chaussettes, les chaussures, les pantoufles,
la casquette, le chapeau, le maillot de
bain

Buying clothes

Est-ce que je peux vous aider? Je cherche (un
manteau). De quelle (taille/pointure/couleur)? En (petite
taille/grande taille/38/taille moyenne/bleu(e)). Est-
ce que je peux l'essayer? C'est trop (grand/petit).
Ça coûte combien? C'est (trop cher/bon
marché). Je ne l'aime pas. Vous l'avez en plus
grand? C'est en (laine/cuir/coton).